THEATRE FOR CHILDREN AND YOUNG PEOPLE

50 years of professional theatre in the UK

PHOTO: SARAH AINSLIE

First printed in 2005 by Aurora Metro Publications Ltd.

Copyright © Aurora Metro 2005

www.aurorametro.com Tel: 020 8898 4488

This publication gratefully acknowledges financial assistance from The Arts Council of England.

Theatre for Children and Young People: Editing and Introduction – copyright © Stuart Bennett 2005

Production: Gillian Wakeling

Trade distribution:

UK – Central Books Tel: 020 8986 4854 Fax: 020 8533 5821 orders@centralbooks.com

USA – Theatre Communications Group, N.Y. Tel: 212 609 5900 info@tcg.org

Canada – Playwrights Union of Canada Tel: 416 703 0013

Printed by Antony Rowe Ltd, Chippenham, UK

ISBN 978-09546912-8-8

THEATRE FOR CHILDREN AND YOUNG PEOPLE

50 years of professional theatre in the UK

edited by Stuart Bennett

with a foreword by Wolfgang Schneider

Casebooks by leading writers, directors and practitioners

- Theatre as an art form experience
- Theatre as an educational force

ASSITEJ

AURORA METRO PRESS

Published in association with ASSITEJ UK
The Association for Children's and Young People's Theatre
as part of the International Series published by ASSITEJ, Germany

Children's and Young People's Theatre in the World
edited by Wolfgang Schneider

For further information see:
www. assitejuk.org
www.kjtz.de

FOREWORD

Children And Young People Need Theatre

Wolfgang Schneider, President of ASSITEJ

Theatre is a contemplation of life. It is a mirror of the times and a stimulus to use one's fantasy in dealing with facts. It is:

- **a medium of social imagination.** Allows recognition, demonstrates and acts out, encourages astonishment and thought; integrates the big, wide world into the small area of the stage. Conflicts and problems are openly discussed. Rebellion can be tried out and anger is not forbidden. Many things are possible on stage. Democratic behaviour and social skills, and, of course, dreams.

- **a school for perception.** Productions are characterised by splendid scenery, or by empty rooms; costumes and masks are used, the little finger plays a role, just like a belt, a violin or a spotlight. Theatre as a code, waiting to be decoded, an aesthetic education.

- **an experience of feelings.** What is friendliness, pleasure, trouble, fear? Alternating hot and cold showers – without getting wet – that's what makes good quality plays. Sharing fear, joy, life. Not because of the feelings, not because of the cheap effects but because of the story being told. Children and young people want to be taken seriously.

- **storytelling in the truest sense of the phrase.** Once upon a time. Lend me an ear. You and me, and we. About a long, long time ago, and about today. In the beginning was the word. In the end is experience. Cryptic stories because children's lives are not all milk and honey, either. That's why both the light and dark sides of stories belong on stage, which means the world.

There is a kind of children's theatre that challenges prejudices for a young audience proving these adults-to-be are more than open to abstract and absurd thinking. The measure for all these things is in the connection between the truthfulness of the acting, and communication between stage actors and audience actors.

CONTENTS

9. ACROSS THE TWO BRANCHES
Art Form and Educational

10. TOURING THEATRE FOR FAMILY
AUDIENCES   239

INTRODUCTION

A HISTORY AND PERSPECTIVE

Theatre for Children and Young People – created and developed by its practitioners.

Stuart Bennett takes you through this development:
- *early history and the two branches*
- *the educational and social context*
- *changing funding patterns*
- *current practice, ideas and issues*

In 2005, ASSITEJ UK set out to survey its practice. A plan was set up by Paul Harman: *how did the movement start, how did it develop, where are we now?* – and importantly – ideas and arguments. Companies and individual directors and writers were invited to contribute. This publication is the result. A wide range of work is reported on, developed not from a conventional model, but from the innovative approaches of its practitioners.

I have organised the material in relation to the two branches of our movement – theatre as an art form experience, and theatre within an educational context. Both reach children and young people in all communities and social groupings. Both have developed work of high quality and originality.

How did the work begin? Retracing our steps will give an idea of why our practice has two branches. It will also map the approaches which continue to underpin the development of new projects. This is not just history – it is the hard-won formulation and testing of practical theatre techniques. Theatre for young audiences has depended as in all countries and cultures on the commitment, skills and initiatives of its practitioners. Let's see how it has worked out here.

The Beginnings

Children's literature developed in European culture in the late nineteenth/early twentieth century. Authors with an understanding of young people's interests began to write specially for them. Stories about young people in school, their friendships and adventures were popular. But theatre provision was very limited: touring companies with dramatisations of folk and fairy tales – *Little Red Riding Hood, Snow White*, and some original adaptations – *The Wind in the Willows, Pinocchio*. The first English children's play, *Peter Pan* (written partly for adults) is an adventure story with a key moment of audience participation – *if you believe in fairies, clap! and Tinker Bell will be saved*.

There was a class context. Repertory theatre was mainly for the middle class. The working class went to popular melodrama and music hall. Crossing this class divide in the Christmas holiday theatre season was the tradition of 'pantomime', a unique English theatre form of popular entertainment for family audiences – the performance of a folk tale (*Cinderella, Aladdin*) as a stage spectacle, combined with music hall, slap-stick and cross-dressing. Its popularity was maintained through the use of participation (cheering the hero, booing the villain). It still is with films such as *Harry Potter* and *The Lord of the Rings* proving to be artistically effective because of the advanced special effects that lift you off your seat – plus the informal atmosphere, popcorn and being able to slip out to the lavatory easily.

However this lack of theatre provision for children and young people was to change radically in the post-war period. It developed – not as the result of a government policy of support for theatre as a form of high culture – but through the insights of key practitioners. What you are about to be taken through may read like a history of our social and educational system – well, that is the context in which we have developed our theatre for children and young people practices. Here goes!

HOW IT BEGAN: Post-war Reconstruction Period

Child-centred Education

The British electorate voted for the Welfare State. The 1944 Education Act had raised the school leaving age to fifteen. There was a move away from traditional rote-learning to 'child-centred education'. This attracted a body of practitioners committed to education as a means of empowering. In schools, instead of sitting in neat rows, children now worked in self-organised groups (influenced by the child-centred approaches of Piaget and Vygotsky). Within this was the recognition of children's creativity.

Child Drama

In many European cultures Child Art had become a recognised area. In Britain there was a parallel movement – *Child Drama* – developed by a children's theatre director, Peter Slade. He observed children playing, and defined two forms. *Personal Play* – where the child runs and chases, and talks to chosen toys. *Projected Play* where children play out a situation – mothers and fathers, cops and robbers, magic spells. His influential book *Child Drama* gave ways for the teacher to develop children's Projected Play into group Creative Drama.

Primary school children come to the school hall. The teacher takes on a role, the leader of an expedition – the children mime exploring a forest, climbing a mountain, someone gets lost and is rescued. Secondary pupils improvise family situations in groups. The teacher takes on appropriate roles to lead the pupils into exploring situations and ideas through drama. Slade used the term Teacher/Actor for the teacher's role, leading pupils into exploring situations and ideas.

Two Key Pioneers

Small professional theatre companies toured dramatisations of children's stories. However there were two directors who saw beyond this and provided the starting point for the big adventure which then ensued. They were the pioneers, and the current two branches can be traced back to their work.

Caryl Jenner and the Unicorn Theatre for Children. A touring theatre director, she was aligned to the Theatre Workshop of Joan Littlewood – taking theatre to the people. She reacted against the limited quality and range of the children's theatre on offer. She set about developing a company which would have a level of truthful playing as authentic as any adult theatre. The company she formed – the Unicorn – toured nationally, then in the 1970's found a base theatre in central London. Plays were commissioned from writers. They were presented on stage with set and design. The Unicorn was the pioneer children's theatre, setting high standards for theatre as an artistic experience. **Tony Graham** follows through this history.

Brian Way and Theatre Centre. He had also been a touring director and had a similar aim. In his case, he had experience of Child Drama. In 1963, he formed Theatre Centre – a collective of actors keen to take on new work. His aim was to reach young audiences directly on a national basis. Therefore he set up a very practical model – four actors touring in a van. The actors' collective had both female and male members. All the company plays were written for a cast of two men and two women. This became significant when the women's theatre movement developed later – companies touring to schools were already equal in gender.

Performances took place in the school hall. The play was presented 'in the round', with no scenery and four classes sitting on the floor round a four-sided performance area. To ensure a close involvement the actors were trained to act the situation – then guide the audience in 'seated participation'. With a younger children's audience they might make a special noise to summon one of the characters, or a special movement to protect the central character from an evil spell. With older pupils they might ask them to advise the main character on what to do.

DEVELOPMENT IN THE WELFARE STATE

Theatre-in-Education

The post-war Labour government had re-structured secondary schools to provide equality of opportunity for all pupils. In addition to child-centred education, the Labour government in the 60's developed the Comprehensive School. Here, instead of selection and grading, pupils were to be taught in mixed-ability classes. It was a democratisation of education, making high quality learning accessible to all. These movements in educational provision contributed to the development of new forms of theatre for young people.

Coventry, a car-manufacturing town in the Midlands – rebuilt its bomb-damaged city centre and opened a new civic theatre, the Belgrade Theatre (named in a spirit of European reconstruction after its twinned city). Plays from the new theatre movement originated at the Royal Court Theatre and were presented on the main stage. In addition, a company of actors was set up to serve the working-class pupils in the city's primary and comprehensive schools. What theatre approach and methods should the company adopt? How best to reach them?

We followed the Theatre Centre model – companies of four, two male, two female, touring schools presenting theatre as a proactive learning experience to widen pupils' horizons. The audience was taken on a journey of discovery. Seated participation was extended into active participatory improvisation workshop sessions. It took the name Theatre-in-Education. Company members had two sets of skills: they were Actor-Teachers.

Classroom Workshop
Typically a TIE day begins with each of the four Actor-Teachers working with a class of pupils in their classroom using drama activities to explore the programme subject area. For example, it was important for the pupils to understand their class position in society in a factory town. The subject for the day, the life of textile workers in the town in the nineteenth century. The classroom drama activity enables them to learn what it is like to be under-paid and exploited. The pupils take on the role of textile factory weavers. The Actor-Teacher first takes on the roles of the factory owner; then of a worker who proposes forming a Trade Union. The pupils have to decide whether to strike or not. This gives them an insight into the real lives of the weavers.

Performance in the Hall
Then the four classes assemble in the hall, sitting on four sides of the square acting area. The Actor-Teachers, now as performers, present a piece of documentary theatre based on research. The pupils as an audience are able to relate to the action, and evaluate it, supported by the learning experience of the drama workshop. The in-the-round presentation, close to the audience, and without scenery is dramatic and authentic. At a key point, the audience participate in role as workers.

Follow-up Session
Each class now returns to their classroom. One of the actors in role as a character in the play sits in front of the class, who are motivated to question the character on feelings and actions. This technique – called 'hot-seating' – proved a very effective participatory method, and is still extensively used. The teacher then takes over, and follows up what they have learned and experienced, about the lives of the factory workers.

The TIE Movement

Companies were set up attached to provincial town Repertory Theatres across the UK: Bolton Octagon, Leeds Playhouse, Watford, Action PIE in Cardiff, Nottingham Roundabout, Peterborough New Perspectives – and in London, Cockpit Theatre, and Greenwich Young People's Theatre. Funding was via the local education authority. The work was carried out in consultation with teachers in schools. It communicated a selected relevant topic. The theatre in performance, and the participatory drama workshop were of a high imaginative standard to communicate relevant learning experience. Above all TIE was a form of empowering the participants' learning.

Drama in Schools

It is also important to relate theatre for children and young people to the context of drama as it developed in schools. Drama and theatre were not introduced as elevated high art – they were part of the active extension of approaches to learning.

Drama-in-Education (DIE)

Pupils exploring experience in role, a form of enactive learning, guided by the teacher. It developed extensively at both primary and secondary school levels – later called 'process drama'. Teachers used it across a range of subject learning areas – what is it like to be someone else? – explored in an open-ended way in role. Carey English refers to the relevance of the work of Dorothy Heathcote – its key teacher – in developing imaginative storytelling with younger children.

Drama as a Curriculum Subject

Secondary school teachers took as their model the Royal Court Theatre. The old-style plays set in country houses had been replaced by Kitchen Sink drama such as *Look Back in Anger*, dealing with contemporary life. Crucially, improvisation became a way of rehearsing dramatic material. This took you away from the text-bound rehearsal of the trained actor into a creative approach. It was seized upon by teachers who found it made theatre accessible to all pupils. 'Push back the desks!' This became the instruction given to the class by the English teacher. In the space provided, pupils explored text through improvisation and devised their own drama.

From this, specialist teachers 'developed', and Drama entered the curriculum as a time-tabled subject.

Where to find the Writers on contemporary themes?

There was now an expansion of Young People's Theatre (YPT). English and Drama teachers wanted their students to see high quality theatre both touring schools and in theatre venues. Theatre Centre continued to tour schools with companies of four, playing in the round. It took on Black and Asian actors and changed from participatory theatre, to a New Writing company, developing new plays on contemporary themes. This is still its policy as Rosamunde Hutt reports. How did the new generation of writers emerge – able to explore and effectively dramatise important social themes and areas of human experience for each age range?

Firstly, they were writers who had learnt their craft in writing the performed play component of TIE participatory theatre. Now they became Young People's Theatre writers in their own right, like Mike Kenny, whose children's plays are widely performed. David Holman recounts the journey he went on as a writer of socially-aware plays. Their great asset was their previous experience of practical school touring, and the educational context for their work. David Wood uniquely took on the challenge of large-scale big touring circuit theatre.

Secondly, they came from the Alternative Theatre Movement. Local education authorities of the major cities and Inner London run by the Labour Party, set up programmes to support Equal Opportunities Policies, organised according to Race, Sex and Class – to promote social equality within schooling. There was a need for writers who could write high quality plays for touring to schools which related to ethnic minority groups, the equal role of women in society – and the culture and rights of the working class.

Women writers were recruited from the women's theatre movement, from companies presenting theatre with a feminist perspective. Plays were written for four actors, two men, two women, and also for all-women companies so the position and viewpoint of women was structurally represented. Theatre Centre continues this with a new generation of women writers.

Black and Asian writers, whose background enabled them to write from their social and cultural position within British society, came into the movement. This is still a proactive area and Dominic Rai reports on a current Asian Theatre Writing Programme.

Special Needs programmes were set up to enable all pupils to participate in theatre experiences. Recent and current practice is described by Oily Cart and Dragon Breath Theatre.

The Politicisation of the Movement

Young People's Theatre companies were politically conscious in their choice of themes. With teacher support, TIE and YPT theatre writers dramatised human situations but with an awareness of the underlying social structures of capitalism. There had been interest in Brechtian Theatre in the 1960's following a visit of the Berliner Ensemble to London. The Alienation/Distancing Effect of Brecht was recreated, but in an educational context. The audience was invited to examine a social situation objectively – not just what is happening, but why. The main gain was the ability to present social/political situations with a clear degree of analysis. The theatre which was created was not didactic – giving the answer. TIE programmes, participatory workshops and documentary theatre were designed to empower the participants, by enabling them to analyse the cause and effect of social and political factors on people's lives.

The Standing Conference of Young People's Theatre

The companies met regularly to share work and debate issues. Companies did not work in isolation – there was a YPT movement and a proactive professional association, SCYPT – the Standing Conference of Young People's Theatre. Companies were funded by local education authorities; they were self-directing. The annual SCYPT conference provided a forum for companies to demonstrate their work for each other, and engage in discussion and appraisal of its principles and effectiveness. This was a very significant facility provided by a self-organised professional body. There were detailed debates and confrontations on a range of political positions but there was a common commitment to empowering young people.

Forum Theatre

Within this context a technique from outside British culture, developed by Augusto Boal in Brazil, was adopted and adapted as a participatory theatre method for social development.

Actors perform a play. It depicts the kind of oppression people in the audience have experienced. Then a Facilitator asks the audience how it could be changed. Members of the audience are invited to take over from the actors the roles of the oppressed in the scene, and to improvise ways for them to change their position in society. This is then discussed by the audience as a group, in a Forum.

Boal worked in Brazil, where there was no tradition of democratic participation. His approach drew on Paolo Freire's *Pedagogy of the Oppressed*, and *Cultural Action for Freedom*. Boal went into exile, came to Europe and re-developed Forum Theatre to counter the internal conditioning of Western society – the 'cop in the head'. How could we be free of the pressures of conformist role-stereotyping for women and men? British companies working within the state education system of a social democracy found Forum Theatre fitted their participatory approaches to developing pupils' political awareness.

An extension of this is Theatre for Development. David Pammenter describes a recent project in the Third World, based on TIE and Forum Theatre techniques.

The Lack of Consistent Funding

Now to a key issue – to try and explain, not justify – why there has never been consistent central government funding for the arts in Britain. This puzzles some European theatre practitioners but that is the reality. The first central funder was the Arts Council, set up under the post-war Labour government, as an independent body to dispense funding 'at arm's length' from government control. When the Conservatives took over, they held back funding. It was 1976 before we had a National Theatre in Britain and it has had to supplement its funding by the transfer of money-making musicals to the West End to balance its books. Theatre in London is largely a commercial operation – cultural tourism.

Funding for theatre for young audiences, as exemplified by Tony Graham's history of the Unicorn Theatre for Children, and David Wood's account of *Whirligig* has followed the same stop-go pattern. This is inconsistent given government commitment to quality services for children. True there has been, and is substantial funding, but allocated as so-called 'core funding' – on the basis that the art form will use it to generate a wider funding base. This keeps the tax-payers happy.

Arts Council core funding to a number of key theatre companies for children and young people has maintained the sector over the years. A large number of other companies obtained the costs of touring to schools by charging fees, which schools then paid from their budgets. This dual funding worked, and it supported a proactive movement for theatre for young audiences during the 70's.

WELFARE STATE TO FREE MARKET ECONOMY

In 1979, the neo-liberal right took over in the form of monetarist policy. Reaganism in the States became Thatcherism in Britain. There was large-scale resistance. Key to this was the role of the Trade Unions. At that time, half the working population were in the manufacturing industries. Theatre companies found themselves living through a period of industrial struggle. During the year-long Miners' Strike of 1984, companies in mining areas were touring schools supervised by police escorts. It was a period when the movement became overtly politicised. Many theatre companies, as trade-unionists, took part in demonstrations, and actively supported the strikes of industrial workers. There were open confrontations within SCYPT between those who adhered to a far-left analysis, the centre left, and non-aligned companies, in terms of political action to defend the gains of the working class.

However it is important to emphasise again that the actual theatre work they toured was not politically didactic, giving the audience the answers. There were Agit-Prop theatre companies like Red Ladder, and the political theatre of 7.84. However that was not TIE/YPT methodology, and as such it would not have been bookable by schools. Although they were politically committed, company practitioners saw themselves as educators, touring socially-aware plays. Theatre and participatory drama were used to set out the issues, to ask the audience to grasp the realities of society – then to respond on their own terms; the aim was to empower – not to indoctrinate.

Education Reform Act

The outcome of the political struggle was that the Conservative government defeated the Trade Unions. The miners marched back to work holding their trade union banners up high, but the industry was doomed. Over the next period the economy changed. The manufacturing base declined rapidly – there was a period of transition as new industries emerged – now two-thirds of the workforce are employed in the service industries, aligned to the global economy. The biggest change that the Free Market government introduced which has had the most direct impact, is the 1988 *Education Reform Act* (ERA). TIE in its original form as a free service ceased to exist.

Local Management of Schools (LMS)

Funding was transferred to each individual school from the local educational authorities who were no longer able to fund companies centrally. Each school became self-managing, and within its limited finances, decided whether it could book touring theatre programmes. Relevance to the National Curriculum became a key factor.

The National Curriculum (NC)

Control of the curriculum was centralised with the aim of assessing standards. Schooling was re-organised into Key Stages 1 and 2 in the primary school; and Stages 3 and 4 in the secondary school. Tested outcomes were introduced at each Key Stage. Literacy, Numeracy and the Core Subjects have to be taught on a set basis in each primary school. In the secondary school the core subjects are Maths, Science and Humanities.

Because of the developed practice of dramatising social issues, and communicating them as theatre experience, many companies found they were able to meet these curriculum requirements. Many schools continued to book – an endorsement of the value and quality of the work. Since this point the movement has been constantly adapting. Theatre for children and young people has undergone continuous redevelopment, without sacrificing its original aims of creating high quality artistic and educational experience.

Association of Professional Theatre for Children and Young People

A new organisation was formed – APT, which set up seminars and conferences to engage the movement with governmental and Arts Council policies. It raised the profile of the movement via a magazine –

Theatre First – dealing with key topics. As the UK ASSITEJ Centre, it maintained and developed key contacts with theatre practices in Europe and the Third World. From this have come important new forms of theatre. Jeremy Turner recounts the value for Welsh companies responding to these contacts to develop culturally.

THEATRE UNDER THE THIRD WAY

New Labour and the Arts and Education

In 1997, New Labour came to power with social regeneration policies. However, there was no return to direct funding. The Conservatives' free market economy was modified and replaced with part-privatisation. The aims of the Welfare State, but funded within an entrepreneurial market economy, the so-called Third Way.

The National Curriculum was seized on as a tool for raising standards of achievement at all pupil levels. Local Management of Schools continues which means that theatre visits have still to be paid out of the individual school budget, related to the delivery of the National Curriculum. They also have to be justified in terms of allocation of curriculum time.

Consequently, theatre now touring to schools and venues can be grouped as follows:.

Theatre by original playwrights

Companies which have core funding from the Arts Council, supplemented by other sources, are able to commission writers to develop plays from their own perceptions and inspirations, relating to children and young people.

Many companies also research the context of the play, say a social theme or personal relationships, and provide an accompanying set of learning resources and activities. These are highly valued by teachers as they enable the pupils to fully assimilate the content, and follow-up the theme of the play. (An example is the teaching videos developed to support Theatre Centre new plays.)

Plays directly related to the curriculum

A subject area within the NC is focussed on. A piece of theatre is presented at a high artistic level which relates to one of the following:

• **Humanities.** This area readily lends itself to exploration through dramatisations related to areas of study in History, Social Studies and Literature. Many companies focus on this context for the themes of the original plays they tour.

- **Science.** Theatre also (perhaps surprisingly) provides an effective way of communicating the principles and practice of scientific thinking. A number of 'theatre for science' companies tour schools.
- **Personal, Social and Health Education.** Also a key component of the National Curriculum is PSHE. This is a learning area, but is not assessed. It is an area where theatre is an ideal means of communication. For example, Y Touring Theatre (funded by the pharmaceutical industry) presented a play telling of the experiences of a young person who becomes mentally depressed. The production was emotionally moving theatre, and effectively raised awareness of what can be done to help.
- **Citizenship.** A New Labour addition to the National Curriculum. Again an area where a dramatisation can often raise awareness more efficiently than a lecture.

Theatre-in-Education programmes (TIE)

TIE approaches continue to operate (though not as a free schools service). Focused on a curriculum learning area the workshop and performance programme gives scope for intensive experience. Anthony Haddon of Theatre Blah Blah Blah describes in-depth TIE work related to primary school literacy.

Within this, there has been a growth of what has been termed 'issue-based' plays and programmes. These can be at a good standard of theatre practice, but are often restricted in the range of areas explored. The ability to 'empower' young people is therefore limited. Ian Yeoman of Theatr Powys makes the distinction.

Life and Social Skills plays

This is also an area that needs to be clarified. There are Life Skills areas that schools need to teach: for instance – road safety. Every day children are killed crossing the road. A lecture will only go so far. An animated theatre presentation can get the message across much more effectively. Schools will therefore pay for a theatre-based teaching session. This is not taking away funding that would otherwise be used for theatre as an artistic experience. It is a recognition by the social agencies of the effectiveness for an audience of watching a situation acted out – as opposed to being given an instructional leaflet.

The Accumulated Assets of the Movement

The reason for detailing the educational and funding context of our theatre practice will now be apparent. The accumulated range of techniques generated in the preceding periods of development, and within educational and social contexts, has now become vitally relevant. Far from junking past techniques and approaches, theatre companies have adapted and reworked them. They are still going through a process of continuous invention. From working within this changing context of social and educational priorities there is a clear commitment to high quality theatre experience for young audiences. Creating theatre is a group practice. Writers, actors and workshop leaders have a common body of skills and methodologies which underpin the movement.

The Two Branches

Leading companies have had to adjust and adapt to the new social realities. Mike Dalton at Popup Theatre, and David Farmer at Tiebreak describe typical changes in company policy and strategies, and movement in company practice across the two branches. They exemplify what characterises our theatre – the ability to explore and communicate personal, social and political issues through a range of effective theatre techniques.

The National Curriculum Updated

Grave concerns began to be expressed by teachers in the 90's that the National Curriculum was teaching basic skills but in a narrow and over-tested context. British education began to revalue creativity as a learning area, and there has been a move to give more flexibility to teachers and pupils to design their own learning plans. An influential report on Creativity was prepared by arts practitioners and educators under the chair of a leading arts academic, Professor Ken Robinson. A funded project, Creative Partnerships, was set up to enable schools in deprived areas to connect with creative arts practice.

Latest Development

New Labour are now reported as linking the next round of arts funding to projects which contribute to local and regional regeneration.

The Director of the Arts Council commented that in terms of the principle of arm's length funding, this new policy would appear to be – 'the Venus de Milo model'. Whatever the outcome, theatre companies will be adept at working to the positive features of this policy.

WHERE WE ARE NOW

The UK is a Federation

There are key reports from Wales – its cultural history, and the range of plays produced by Theatr Cymri Arad Goch; from Scotland on the impact of its own festival, Imaginate; from Replay Productions on working creatively within Northern Ireland's social and political context. Their work has developed within the overall UK pattern, but with their own approach, as funding has become progressively more devolved.

Regeneration

There are also funded initiatives to regenerate regional areas. Currently, there is movement in Regional Theatres to involve young people and schools in a wide range of projects as outlined by Birmingham Rep and The Sherman Theatre. These include developing community audiences, as related by Man Mela and Jack Drum Arts. And in London, Tony Graham outlines the potential for the new Unicorn to provide a focus for developments.

The Process of Creative Theatre

We have followed through theatre development in the educational and funding context. Within this, theatre companies have developed a wide and creative range of theatre as both an art form experience, and as a learning experience. The focus now – at last! – shifts specifically to the creation of quality theatre for children and young people. Here the practitioners outline their creative practices in action! Polka, Vicky Ireland, Travelling Light and Classworks take you inside this exciting process. David Wood and David Holman describe the range of their writing.

International Contacts

The theatre of the English culture is actors conveying human situations through the power and subtlety of language. In Elizabethan times you went to the Globe Theatre 'to hear the players' – not 'to see the play.' Many UK practitioners can recount mind-opening experiences from international contacts.

A performance in a theatre in Moscow with a young audience. The servant in a land-owner's household is blind. His faithful companion is his dog. The mistress of the house however commands him to drown it. He picks up a real trained dog, holds it in his arms – walks downstage – light conveys the reflections over the river – (a trap opens and the dog disappears) – then the sound of rushing water and the whimpering of the dog. He weeps.

So did everyone in the audience; you could not but be moved by the physical reality. It opened up creative staging for me.

As practitioners we have been inspired by this range of theatre at Assitej Congresses. Paul Harman gives examples. At the Take-off Festival we have seen international work which communicates aesthetic experiences for children. Playtime recount developing practical cross-Europe exchanges. Henning Fangauf reports on plays by our writers in the repertoire of young people's theatre companies in Germany.

So international reader – here's a deal. Show us how theatre is created in your culture and we will learn from it – and borrow effective techniques. In return, we can teach you a range of approaches to theatre as a proactive social force. Please borrow and adapt.

Key Characteristics of the Movement in the UK

Downside: the constant need to re-negotiate base funding from diverse sources; currently a combination of Arts Council, limited-term government initiatives, local government grants, charitable trusts, and for the last ten years the National Lottery.

Positive side: the need to be proactive has led to a diversity of theatre forms and practices in a wide range of contexts. Key to this is the development of high quality theatre for young people in the context of their social, cultural and educational development. This actively includes the wide range of ethnic diversity in the UK.

The two branches, as art form and educational force, are parallel, but interact creatively. Underpinning the descriptions of past and current practice is the diversity of theatre as performance and as educational force, both contributing to the social awareness of a new generation. There has been a cross-over movement in recent years. Practitioners describe how the original TIE practice has been subsumed into a wider arts practice – a meeting in the middle.

Achieving and maintaining access is a key aim:

– for children of all social classes through touring to schools
– for children in the family context through local community venues

Conclusion

The contributions we have included are a response to a call to companies to report on company histories, current practice and what they see as key issues. They are to inform you the reader – and to share practice across the movement. We need to review the key current issues as much as you! Theatre work is highly valued in terms of child development, and the social and cultural development of young people. While we will continue to campaign for proactive central funding, the ability of the movement to create innovative work will continue.

Paul Harman's plan for this publication included active debate and argument. Within these pages practitioners offer continuous practical reassessment of the relationship between performance and workshops. There is much to be gleaned from this. This collection is not an archive of the past – it is a blueprint for the next phase of development. Join in the Debate!

Stuart Bennett was a member of the pioneer TIE company at Coventry Belgrade Theatre. He set up the first professional training for actors working with children and young people, and as Director of Cockpit Theatre was active in theatre for, and with young people in inner London.

DRAMA ACTIVITY IN SCHOOL

Improvising in role (Roundabout TIE)

YOUTH THEATRE

Young people meeting in their own time to rehearse and perform a play

1. DEVELOPMENTS IN THE UK

THEATRE FOR YOUNG PEOPLE IN WALES

First, Eirwen Hopkins on the emergence of a Welsh theatre, the setting up of Theatre-in-Education companies, the breakaway from the English movement, and the establishment of a new network in Wales.

Theatre in the Land of Coal and Culture

A country of four million, with three cities around the coast. Among the hills and valleys lurks the physical – and cultural legacy of heavy industries, once the *raison d'etre* of these communities. Rows of Victorian terraced houses along the hill slopes. Outside the coal seams and once-busy port areas are market towns and villages, dependant on farming and tourism. A dominant heritage of Puritanism. A strong cultural identity with choral groups travelling over the hills to entertain their neighbouring communities.

Mainstream theatre existed in the form of the English repertory theatre system. Then in the early 70's, came a drive to give the Welsh the theatre they deserved. New buildings were erected, old ones refurbished. Community companies were funded to tour new material to the small towns and villages. By the time I started working in theatre in Wales in 1974, many things seemed possible. Theatre was actively branching out. Theatre which challenged, explored and redefined the actor-audience relationship.

A Proactive Welsh TIE Movement

Education advisers set up Theatre-in-Education (TIE) companies in Clwyd, North West Wales and Powys, East Wales, along with Youth Theatre companies. Members of the original Coventry TIE company set up Action Projects in Education in Cardiff, Gwent TIE and with my own group Open Cast Theatre in Swansea, teaching us to experiment and improvise. In fact, Welsh companies became key to TIE as a movement in Britain, and were active within the national movement SCYPT (Standing Conference of Young People's Theatre).

Of four million people, about an eighth speak Welsh, and prefer to operate on a daily basis through the medium of their native tongue. There is an ancient and profound tradition behind the language and its culture. By the end of the 70's, we perceived the need for work to take place in Welsh. Those aware of the threats to our cultural bio-diversity campaigned, within and outside official institutions, to establish recognition and respect for the minority culture. My company didn't work in Welsh, so I moved to the new Theatr Crwban. TIE using Welsh gives children an incentive to think laterally, to understand – and it has the practical effect of enthusing children about their language.

A Welsh – not English Theatre

By the 80's, Welsh theatre found a popular form for modern audiences with elements from its own true culture. Then Cardiff Laboratory Theatre brought in fresh air from Europe and the East. We saw Odin Teatret, Grotowski, Kathakali. These influences fed into the work. We were excited by the idea that we could create something which spoke directly without the cultural baggage that English forms brought with them. We experimented with stylised work, non-narrative and physical theatre. We welded these elements with indigenous forms to bring into being a new kind of popular theatre. A Welsh theatre company, Theatr Bara Caws (Bread and Cheese Theatre) had been set up in the mountainous Nort-speaking company – Cwmni'r Frân Wen. An Experimental Theatre and TIE group formed to become what is now a key contemporary company – Cwmni Theatr (Welsh Theatre) Arad Goch.

However by the 90's, the Thatcher Government brought matters of funding to a crisis. On a national basis, funding by local education authorities, key to the artistic independence of companies, was transferred to individual schools. Local government in Wales was reorganised with eight authorities being replaced by twenty-three small ones. This swept away co-ordinated funding for theatre for schools as a free service. We were now competing within school budgets against educational necessities. In the context of the political fight against financial cut-back some SCYPT companies saw developing theatre related to a minority language and culture as irrelevant. This led to disagreement, and the Welsh language companies withdrew.

A New Welsh Network

With support from the Welsh Arts Council, the Welsh companies survived – more than survived. They continued to develop, experiment and produce work of quality. Each company found its own answers to its funding crisis: some reduced their casts, some offered alternative services to schools, others toured the world. They maintained a level of creative energy, and were not contained by the requirement of the new National Curriculum. They commissioned new work, developed educational practice and increased their profile in the community. These eight companies now serve all parts of Wales. Director-led, or co-operatives, each company has its own priorities – region, educational development, Welsh performance style – a combination of these.

We now have a devolved Welsh government, introduced in 1998, which looks to be injecting new funding, and a new sense of pride and energy into the work. The original keystone of TIE policy, a service free to schools, has been re-instated as a long term aim. The eight companies now have a chance to work for the future, and drive their own creative force towards rediscovering their past: both in terms of their cultural traditions and language, and their roots in the TIE movement. It's an exciting time.

Eirwen Hopkins was a founder member of Open Cast Theatre and Theatr Crwban, and Director of Cwmni'r Frân Wen.

YOUNG PEOPLE'S THEATRE IN A MINORITY LANGUAGE AND CULTURE

Jeremy Turner takes up the story of the development of theatre for young people in a minority language and culture.

Minority Language and Culture Rights

At the 1993 ASSITEJ Congress in Cuba, we heard much discussion about the role theatre plays in strengthening and confirming children's and young people's sense of identity and belonging. We heard from every continent about traditional myth and folk-art used to reaffirm cultural heritage; we heard about the use of contemporary idioms in order to recognise and respect young audiences' awareness of their own identity. We also heard about the role language plays – one's mother-tongue or family language, with its delicate network of accumulated associations, and untraceable connections, is our link to the past and to our society. It is at the heart of our sense of belonging and is the passport to our identity. The *UN Convention of the Rights of the Child, Article 30*, states that a child belonging to an ethnic, religious, linguistic or indigenous minority should be able to 'enjoy their own culture, to use his or her own language.' To promote the rights and identity of our young audiences worldwide, it was proposed that we recognise minority cultures, and promote theatre for young audiences in lesser-known languages.

These sentiments were familiar to me. ASSITEJ-UK had discussed the need to promote theatre for young audiences in their own languages, to facilitate and strengthen the role those young people play in a wider society. As a practitioner of theatre in Wales, with its own indigenous culture and language, I know from experience that such an aim was easy to discuss but sometimes difficult to put into practice. Wales almost lost its own language, and this may be why there is now an increasing awareness of its importance as a key to cultural heritage and a sign of contemporary identity. Wales, like many other countries, accepts the advantages of bi and multilingualism. Children are now able to receive their education through Welsh; books, newspapers and periodicals are published in the language, and there are Welsh language television and radio channels.

However, there remains the tendency and danger, towards insularity. Many minority cultures and languages are often isolated from a wider cultural context both by the dominant culture of the state – and by their own sense of inferiority. This had been the case in Wales where Welsh culture has been hidden in the shadow of its dominant neighbour. To many people, both abroad and within the UK – 'England' and 'The United Kingdom' are synonymous. We have for some time, realised the importance of providing wider contexts for our work. An isolated and insular culture is a culture in danger or even, a dangerous culture. A culture within a wider context can be both rooted – and progressive. Ironically, whilst many 'majority' cultures are worrying about the loss of their own individuality within rootless generic Euro-Americanism, some minority cultures are now re-establishing their identity.

Development of a Welsh Approach

Theatre in Wales had developed as part of the mainstream of conventional, narrative, naturalistic or neo-naturalistic Western-European theatre. The last thirty years, have seen exploration of alternative forms, styles, techniques and content for 'accessible experimentation' (as opposed to a decline in British 'experimental theatre').

Many theatre practitioners in Wales in the 80's and 90's, purposely avoided contemporary English influence, turning to the work of European practitioners. The work and ideas of Ray Nusselein of Paraplyteatret and other colleagues in Denmark and Belgium, had a strong effect on a number of Welsh children's theatre workers, and helped us to re-assess our own criteria. We found a freedom of expression and creativity in the experimental, physical and visual trends of theatre in continental Europe and in other cultures; the work and ideas of Barba and Grotowski had a strong influence enabling us to challenge conventions and expectations.

Much use has been made of the juxtaposition of traditional material and performance forms with contemporary styles. Arad Goch's production of *Taliesin* (1995-99) succeeded on foreign stages because of its fusion of something specific to Wales (a Sixth Century epic tale), with contemporary performance techniques. The imagistic tradition of Welsh literature has been transposed into a contemporary theatrical idiom, which has added to the strength of new writing in both languages. Contemporary Welsh language writers draw on Welsh literary tradition, transposing and often challenging it, to create reflections of modern Wales.

The merging of these apparently opposing elements, traditional and contemporary, has resulted in a hybrid contemporary, indigenous Welsh theatre, including Theatre-in-Education. The ability of children and young people to accept any form of high standard artistic presentation has aided the exploration of new forms of theatre. The proximity to our audience, and co-operation with teachers, and other educationalists constantly encourage us to question our own values and the content, style and standard of our work.

Working in Bilingual and Monolingual Contexts

Matters of content which can be taken for granted in a 'safe' or main-language culture, are amplified in a minority context. Bilingual and monolingual young people share the same country, culture, and education system but the social and cultural reference points for each group often differ. This is an essential point for international exchanges; a performance which makes perfect sense in its own context can seem self-indulgent, or old-fashioned in another. Bilingual Welsh/English young people have a greater awareness of and pride in their own Welsh/Celtic cultural heritage, a greater awareness of cultural diversity, and an easier acceptance of multilingualism than their monolingual friends.

As Welsh is a 'minority' language, it is understandable that the bilingual Welsh/English speaking children are in a dilemma about the place of their culture in a wider society. For these children, theatre based on their own heritage (legends, stories and history), is a way to reinforce their own identity. But caution is needed: the use of such material can lead to a perpetuation of sentimental cultural stereotypes. More fruitful is the use of traditional source material – but within a non-traditional or de-constructed style.

The monolingual English speaker's awareness of Welsh identity is often based on more obvious and nationalistic symbols of identity (the annual Patron Saint's day, the national rugby team), and less on immediate experience and knowledge of traditional cultural heritage and practice. It is also based on recent industrial working-class culture and background. Though monolingual English speakers are no more or less Welsh than their bilingual friends, they are usually more aware of English than Welsh culture – or are torn between their Welsh identity and the Anglo-American identity imposed upon them by the dominant culture of the British Isles. For these children, theatre based on Welsh material, historical or contemporary, is a way to reintroduce cultural heritage – so reinforcing the child's awareness of and pride in his or her own identity. But equally important for these children, is theatre which enables them to see themselves, their culture and their country as part of a wider European and world perspective.

Identity and a Wider Perspective

This is of immense importance to the development and stability of any culture in crisis. It is at the very root of our thinking as we create theatre for young audiences who want both to belong and to rebel, to conform and to be different. Multi-culturalism can only exist when each individual culture (whatever its size), is allowed by the internal and external contexts in which it operates, to develop freely and to function in a way relevant to its own audience. It would be interesting to compare bilingualism in theatre in Wales with that of other countries with minority languages. A Welsh-speaking teenager in a small town in West Wales called out to the actors of the theatre company visiting the school – "You're our company aren't you!" The value of our work enhances young people's sense of ownership of contemporary theatre presented to them on their terms, and with relevance to their own cultural context.

Themes in the Cwmni Theatr Arad Goch repertoire

- Each of the plays is rooted in Welsh culture – but also challenges the status quo of that culture in its style, or content, or both.
- Each operates irrespective of linguistic or political bias – offering young audiences a positive perspective on the use, and value of their contemporary culture.
- The company's work is concerned with the development of a culture, rather than with its sterile preservation.

Plays with a historical theme

The Good Brig Credo By Mari Rhian Owen, set in nineteenth century West Wales, is an adventure story about escaping, travelling and

finding new horizons. The historical backdrop gives cultural depth and objectivity to an exposition of social injustice. The rich use of language – colloquial dialogue, more lyrical structured poetry and folk songs and music – with strong visual staging.

First sight of the new world

Plays for Children

Dros y Garreg (Over the Stone) by Mari Rhian Owen, a play for small children, set in its own enclosed environment and written for an actress, a puppet and a musician, is about the loneliness that some children face when they are unable to conform to accepted conventions. The script makes use of nursery rhymes and folk music.

Y Sied (The Shed) by Mari Rhian Owen is a play for children about old people and death. The play is set in a garden shed, where three old people meet to escape loneliness, reminisce, play jokes on each other, argue, and face the coming darkness together.

Plays for Teenagers

Confetti (Confetti) by Sêra Moore Williams is about sibling rivalry, nihilism and an all too common senseof hopelessness. Minimalist scenography and live guitar music contribute to one of the most powerful new plays in Wales. Two estranged brothers meet again at their father's second wedding – and things are no better.

Riff by Sêra Moore Williams addresses the advent of gun culture to the UK and deals with one boy's reaction to the Columbine tragedy in the USA. Strongly influenced by work with

Youth from *Riff*

disaffected young people, with direct relevance to contemporary youth culture in Wales.

Technology and Theatre for Young Audiences

Sêra Moore Williams' work as a director makes much use of technology, live music and projection of static and moving imagery. Her paper presented at the ASSITEJ Congress in Seoul 2002, was published in *Technology for Children's Theatre*, Challenge or Risk by ASSITEJ Korea. Jeremy Turner's recent production of *Caneri, Gwylan a Brân* (*Canary, Seagull and Crow*) was commissioned by the National Library of Wales to launch its new multi-media auditorium.

The play takes three events in Welsh history as part of the story-line in the journey of an insecure, unconfident young girl – with each event enabling her to realise her own potential. The objectivity of the events was contrasted with the harshness and immediacy of the use of video, digital imagery and a sound-track of guitar music.

The girl reads her Welsh history

Jeremy Turner is Director of Theatr Arad Goch. He is ASSITEJ UK's International Representive.

REVIVAL OF THEATRE IN SCOTLAND – The Cinderella Story of Scottish Children's Theatre

Tony Reekie accounts for the upturn in Children's Theatre in Scotland. The sharing and promotion of work at the Imaginate Festival has had a regenerating impact.

Funding for Children's Theatre

In 2003, Children and Young People's Theatre in Scotland appeared to have made a breakthrough. Scotland has an independent Executive and Arts Council: both bodies had endorsed the idea of entitlement to culture as being at the heart of growing up, and a commitment to investment in that process. But this is Scotland – a nation who snatch defeat from the jaws of victory. Scratch at the surface and get a different take on events. The Scottish Arts Council decided that all the children's companies would start on a level playing field – £130,000 for five core-funded companies. However, TAG, the only dedicated company for children and young people in the list, received a reduction of 50%. Two steps forward and one and half back in terms of central funding. Paradoxically, Imaginate Children's Theatre Festival is now the highest funded performing arts organisation in Scotland (through sponsorship by the Bank of Scotland), but we don't actually originate any theatre work ourselves.

The Festival

To explain the success of new Scottish work, the Imaginate Children's Theatre Festival has to be acknowledged. Prior to 1990, with the exception of TAG and occasional work by companies like Communicado, the quality of work in Scotland was poor. The work was cheap, under-produced, under-rehearsed, variations on pantomime with enough audience participation to keep the audiences from catching breath to realise what rubbish it all was.

Imaginate Children's Theatre Festival landed into this wasteland of theatrical pain and misery in 1990, and slowly began to change the outlook of new artists coming into the area. For the first time in Scotland we could look at the best the world had to offer – work of the highest standard, that time and time again made us gasp with its passion, skill and daring. What also helped was the environment of the festival: a sharing of ideas and talent, a place where people came together and talked, agreed, disagreed and argued into the small hours about work. This was a way of working that we hadn't tried before, and it forced artists in Scotland to raise their game, to question the how and why about their own work.

Creators quickly moved away from the National Curriculum, and from trying to second guess the education system, to tell the stories they wanted to tell. In an instant, this freed up the creative process and meant that the companies were leading the way in terms of subject matter, rather than responding to the education system and funding bodies. 'Issues' at long last were out, or were at least only a part of an artistic process that aimed to thrill, move and entertain its audience. We now have high quality productions in Scotland, enjoying success throughout the world, and some of them still touring four or five years after their initial run.

The Companies

Each of the companies has developed in its own way, resulting in a body of work that is highly diverse.

Wee Stories have taken interactive storytelling to new heights. Their productions talk directly to the audience and allow them to participate, but in a way that never feels forced. One memory stands out for me at the Festival – a performance of *Labyrinth*, their story of the Golden Fleece (5+). At one moment the audience, and chorus, were gently swaying as the sea, unprompted. A German company sat intent at the back. At the end, they rushed up saying how skilled the piece was in telling the story, and letting the audience become part of the whole event. It had that effect on everyone.

Catherine Wheels and **Visible Fictions** have both developed a style of theatre not relying on the spoken word. Theatre in Scotland previously had the time-honoured way of producing – writer in turret, director moves actors around to desired effect. This company has found new ways to tell a story theatrically.

Martha by Catherine Wheels is the story of an old woman who lives alone and is visited by a goose.

PHOTO: ROBERT WORKMAN

Goose arrives

The Red Balloon, by Visible Fictions is an adaptation of the famous book and movie about the little boy befriended by a balloon. I remember at the Take Off Festival, a child about eighteen months old standing up, watching in rapt attention the whole way through.

Both scripts are basically stage directions. What both productions have developed is an almost silent-movie approach to story-telling, with visuals, movement and music, conveying the story. These are both stories about people who are seeking friendship; both aimed at a relatively young audience (4/5 years) and both have the ability, at every per-formance I've seen, to have the audience in tears. These are genuine family shows in the truest sense of the word. Not relying on the written word meant that the companies had to search for the right theatrical expression for a scene, or an action. They were encouraged by the international work that fully utilised all that theatre has to offer to convey its message – music, movement, puppetry, lighting became narrative tools. This works with a children's audience happy to embrace a fully sensual theatre experience.

Shona Reppe. *Cinderella* – in one sense this show could be seen as encompassing all the good things about work in Scotland. Small, beautifully conceived, slightly camp, an absolute joy from start to finish. The Ugly Sisters trying on Cinderella's slippers with a chainsaw was a personal favourite. It encapsulates for me what is good about children's theatre in Scotland, and good children's theatre anywhere. Artists following their own paths, finding out what passions drive them, putting their visions on stage. They follow no agenda other than their own: no educational, social, demands that place the issue above the story or the human beings, and kill theatre stone dead.

TAG Theatre. Founded in the 60's. Stephen Greenhorn and David Greig have explored themes of citizenship, nationhood, and the rights of children. *Dr Korczak* (11+), the true story of a Jewish orphanage in Warsaw in the Second World War was a measured, thoughtful work that packed a punch which left its audience reeling.

I'm not suggesting that these developments were only happening in Scotland but as a small country, it was easier for the creation of pieces I have mentioned to be seen as a movement, and a new force in the artistic community. On the back of this work we were able to argue for greater resources, for family-friendly venues, for an emphasis on more and better work, for children around Scotland, and, finally – we always do things back to front – for greater central funding for those producing that work.

Dr Korzak

'Imaginate' Development

From a tented village in the centre of Edinburgh, (smashing idea for when the rain pours down, as it did with monotonous regularity) – we have gone on to utilising Edinburgh's best theatre venues and placing high quality children's performing art from around the world at the heart of the theatre community. We have increased the number of delegates from five in 1995 to over one hundred and forty in 2004. As well as this we try, with varying degrees of success, to continue a general discussion about the work we do. Our organisation has changed too, and under its new guise of Imaginate, we have a broader role to promote and develop performing arts for children and young people in Scotland.

- We now run our own showcase, *What You See is What You Get* (WYSIWYG), an idea stolen from Take Off, thanks to Paul Harman and the CTC team. This travels around Scotland every year and is an opportunity for our community to come together, see work, and get slightly inebriated. We tour international work all over Scotland.

- We have a skills development programme in which we encourage new and established practitioners to develop their own skills through visits abroad, seminars, and workshops.
- We have a Development Manager who has overseen the creation of a website: **www.family-friendly.net/home**.
- We have started discussion with cultural co-ordinators on assessing quality, and how to be an effective catalyst between schools and companies. This work culminated in the publication of *A Stage Further*, and a conference alongside the Children's Festival.

Other organisations like the Puppet and Animation Festival have recognised the need for puppet companies to have access to directorial or dramaturgical support in the creation of their work. They have set up a small, but highly effective fund, whereby puppet companies can bring in the practitioners of their choice to assist in the creation of new work.

Onwards and Upwards?

The general success of the festival, along with the work coming out from the top companies, has encouraged us to believe that children's theatre in Scotland is perhaps the success story of the past decade.

And, of course, we need to move forward. It's great that after so many years, some companies finally have funding. £130,000 per company is, of course, not enough, but it does at least allow for some kind of stability. We also have the perennial issue of new talent, and the creation of a sector that looks inviting enough to entice people in the first place. Our top companies can be very good, but we need a steady and developing flow of ideas and approaches. One area Imaginate is working in, is the development of courses in theatre for children and young people, to encourage understanding and develop a passion for the work, while students are still at college or university. This has had some effect already, and there are a number of young companies coming through.

It's up to us to make sure that they can flourish within a well-resourced framework for the benefit of both Scottish Theatre and the audience.

Tony Reekie is Director of Imaginate International Children's Theatre Festival (Bank of Scotland).

THEATRE FOR YOUNG PEOPLE IN NORTHERN IRELAND

Richard Croxford recounts the social, cultural and political context of Replay's work in a divided community.

Award-winning Replay Productions is a professional educational theatre company based in Belfast. Established in 1988, Replay is dedicated to providing high quality theatre that entertains, educates and stimulates children and young people of all abilities, and to supporting and inspiring the adults that work with, and care for them. The company tours to schools and venues throughout Northern Ireland. All projects provide unique curriculum support, encourage increased understanding, development and learning (both at school level and in life skills) and promote concepts of cultural identity and diversity.

Northern Ireland has few providers other than Replay with a specific remit of theatre and drama for young people. The company has been supportive of new companies which have evolved over the last couple of years such as Cahoots NI, Theatre Oomph, Ababu and Colonel Von Trapp's Puppets, as it is keen to see theatre for young audiences develop and share good practice with its peers. Theatre for young people forms an element of the programme of a number of touring companies (Big Telly Theatre Company, Bruiser Theatre Company, The Armagh Rhymers, Sole Purpose Productions, Tinderbox). In the main theatres (Lyric Theatre and Grand Opera House), provision for young people is confined mostly to either seasonal productions – Christmas pantos or summer musicals, or the production of school curriculum texts – Shakespeare, O'Casey, etc.

The establishment of the 'Young At Art Children's Cultural Festival' in 1998, has had a significant impact on the profile of arts for children and young people, both in theatre and other art forms.

How 'Replay' began

In the late 1980's, when Replay was set up, much of Northern Ireland's independent theatre had evolved out of the Troubles, but then a new wave of theatre practitioners sought to explore and express a different side of Northern Ireland.

Brenda Winter, founder: There were two things that impelled me to form Replay. I can trace the first directly to a night when I sat, as an unemployed actress, in the Lyric Theatre and experienced the excitement of what was the first night of Martin Lynch's *Dockers*. For the first time I realised that the accent I spoke with, and the place I came from, was as valid and exciting as anything I had ever seen represented on stage to date, a celebration of a specifically Northern Irish identity. The second reason was to do with my close connection to education. In a short detour before I opted for the less secure option of a life in the theatre, I had trained and worked as a teacher. In my early career as an actress, I had also been part of ad hoc companies of actors who had 'gotten up' a little show to take round schools, a lucrative and captive market, since properly organised and funded Theatre-in-Education had collapsed here in the mid 80's. The production standards of these companies were often lamentable, operating as they did without subsidy on a profit-share basis. Young people in schools in Northern Ireland were not getting what they deserved, in a context that reflected their own experience.

The story of Replay is one of being in the right place at the right time. The seed funding came from Belfast City Council who just happened to be looking for an event to commemorate the centenary of Belfast as a city, when the company was preparing *Under Napoleon's Nose*, a play on the history of Belfast. (Napoleon's Nose being Belfast's most famous local geographical landmark, a hill which seen from the city below looks like the shape of a man's head; it was this giant man's head that was the inspiration for *Gulliver's Travels, and his adventures in Lilliput*.)

Education for Mutual Understanding

The next break for Replay was to be 'noticed' by a very discerning civil servant who recognised the potential of theatre to promote better community relations. At the time 'Education For Mutual Understanding and Promotion of Cultural Heritage' (EMU) was a major priority in government policy. Funding opportunities previously unavailable to arts groups were opened to us. This was a huge milestone in the development of the company, and we didn't have to make any compromises to fit the bill. It became a cross-curricular theme in schools, and as such linked into all aspects of the curriculum.

While the term, EMU and Cultural Heritage, is unique to Northern Ireland, the ideas behind them can be found in many educational systems around the world, not least in countries, or regions, where there is, or has been communal conflict. Wherever it is found, or whatever it is called, such work reflects an educational concern to help children and young people to understand and respect human diversity, to develop skills in personal and group relationships, and to deal creatively with conflict. EMU/Cultural Heritage was fundamentally about affirming the richness of human diversity and helping people to learn to live with their differences in a spirit of acceptance and mutual respect. Easy then to see how Replay's work fitted in so well here, with the intention of helping young people to build those bridges of understanding, respect and acceptance through creative means.

It is interesting to note that for much of the early part of the 'Troubles' in the 70's, schools were seen as a safe haven, a protected environment where the violence and communal conflict were excluded. Teachers often saw their role as one of limiting discussion of controversial issues, and preventing the outbreak of dissension in their oasis of peace. For many young people, this provided the only stability in an otherwise turbulent landscape. The arts were also used in this way.

Neil Martin, a local musician: With the advantage of hindsight, I now know that what music offered – especially through those very dark days of the 1970's when all hell was breaking loose in the real world of the north – was a sanctuary, a safe house, where, for a few hours each week, we were cocooned in this other world of communications, where we had this common language that we did not even once tarnish or sully with religion or politics. We developed relationships that remain steadfast in our lives. We grew up through music and, at least in part, because of it. Music didn't solve any political problem, but it allowed us at one and the same time to express feelings, tapped and untapped, and for a while to forget what was going on around us. Without a doubt it saved many of us from lives much less savoury.

Gradually, within the education system an appreciation grew of the responsibility to face the challenges presented by the conflict in a more proactive way, which is why EMU, and collaborations between young people, and many arts organisations evolved. It did not enjoy universal support, and there were those, on both sides of 'the divide', who saw it as social engineering driven by a desire to dilute cultural identity. EMU was a bold initiative which helped to change the nature of discourse in Northern Ireland by introducing a language that 'allows people to express their support for cultural pluralism and political dialogue, rather than sectarianism and political violence' (Smith and Robinson, 1996). Their report *Towards a Culture of Tolerance: Education For Diversity* (DENI, 1999) recognised that EMU and other initiatives: "have had considerable success in breaking down barriers, opening people's minds and establishing new networks of contacts. However, it is not surprising that, in the face of centuries-long social divisions, they must be seen as merely the beginning of social transformation."

Pupil Contact in Workshop Sessions

Numerous schools used EMU initiatives to pay for Replay, and other arts organisations, to visit their school. With Replay this usually meant that two school groups from across the divide were brought together, either at a neutral venue, or one of the group's schools, to see a show or participate in a joint workshop. Sadly, a lot of the time when they came to see a production, the two groups sat separately, and did not have the opportunity to mix, or discuss what they had just seen – a tragic waste, and so not what EMU was all about.

The Workshop Programme however worked well, with sessions where teachers got the groups to mix, and discuss the play afterwards. The young people would always be wary at the start, but once some of their inhibitions died down they would realise they had vast amounts in common, and that the 'opposition' didn't really have ten heads and go around eating babies, as was the previous impression. Today when speaking to people who were involved in these schemes when they were younger, one finds that they can all remember not only aspects of the production or workshop, but their first meeting with a 'Teague' (derogatory term for a Catholic), or 'Hun' (derogatory term for a Protestant).

A New Era

Since the cessation of military operations by paramilitaries, and the devolution of Northern Ireland, it would appear the province is moving from a situation of conflict into a new political era. In the light of past experience with programmes such as EMU, the Education System in Northern Ireland is seeking to find ways of supporting moves towards democracy, and to find alternatives both to violence and to avoidance of discussion of issues which divide us. The Northern Ireland Curriculum (CCEA, 1999) states the intention to introduce a programme of citizenship education, because of the responsibility the education system has 'to contribute towards the maintenance of peace'.

It is refreshing then to hear from Michael Arlow of CCEA (Council for Curriculum Examinations and Assessment). It would seem appropriate that the members of this society are educated in such a way as to facilitate their involvement in the transformation of their society, and to deal critically and creatively with the realities of past events, the difficulties of the present situation, and the hopes and aspirations of all as we carve out a new future. We are starting to think beyond a utilitarian concept of education as producing adults to conform to the defined norms of society, and to consider a definition of education that affords individuals the opportunity to become agents of change.

Our Three Year Strategy

With new social issues dawning on the back of the ceasefire, most notably racism, it is essential for arts organisations such as Replay to assist with those opportunities. The arts, as we practitioners are so vividly aware, are also very well placed to assist teachers and youth leaders to develop their skills of cultural exploration. To better place Replay as an agent of change, the company devised its first three year strategy in 2001. The strategy identified the company's mission as – providing high quality professional theatre that entertains, educates and stimulates children and young people.

The strands of work the company under4take are:

- **Theatre on the Road.** This is the main element of the company's work; full quality theatre productions. At least 50% of the company's work is new commissions. The company visits nursery, primary, secondary and special schools with audiences ranging from three to eighteen. There is no set style, although productions over the last four years have been physical and visual with strong scripts, some funny and wacky, some intense and tragic, and a varied form of staging including promenade, thrust and end on. Audience sizes in schools are eighty to a hundred pupils, and tours are normally nine weeks duration.

- **Theatre in a Rucksack.** These are mini-productions where everything (set, costume, props) is supposed to fit into a rucksack (the reality is a car boot.) The idea for these productions evolved out of the company receiving so many requests to revive shows, and to tour outside of the province. It is also an ideal medium for working with the very young (3 to 5's).

- **Theatre Squad.** These are theatrical stand-alone workshops which use elements of theatre to explore topical issues affecting the youth of today, e.g. bullying/peer pressure, anger management/emotional control, racism/discrimination etc. It is hoped this will provide the company with topical participatory work available all year round, and access areas other Replay projects cannot.

- **Theatre Masterclass.** A programme of workshops and training sessions to develop, and enhance the skills of local artists in producing theatre, and related activities, for young audiences.

- **Theatre-in-Residence.** Residency programmes to explore issues through artistic media. These have been two/three day, week-long and year long and evolved out of our strong tradition of special schools work. They are still used in special schools, but rather than be stand-alone workshop projects, they are now used to support Replay's creative programme enabling youngsters with physical and learning disabilities to gain the maximum benefit from productions. They are also now being used in primary and secondary schools to explore methods of improving behaviour.

- **Theatre on Site.** The company has a long history of site-specific work particularly at historical sites around Northern Ireland. The expense of these productions has prohibited the company producing them over the last few years. However there are plans for a promenade version of *Macbeth* in the gloomy chambers of the Lagan Lookout, underneath the river Lagan that runs through Belfast.

Presenting Theatre across the Sectarian Divide

With the political and social situation here in Northern Ireland, our productions must also be relevant to both sides of the community. There are numerous symbols of religion throughout the province. For example, where you live in a city can instantly tell someone which faction you belong to. As a vast generalisation, the middle classes live in the mixed areas of the city, and the working classes in segregated areas. Schools are generally of one denomination. There are a number of integrated schools evolving, but most of these are in middle-class areas where people are socially mixed anyway.

Some areas of Belfast have road signs in Irish, and the tricolour flag flying, others have pavements painted red, white and blue, and the Union Jack flying. Whether you play Gaelic football (Catholic) or Rugby (Protestant), the way you speak e.g. correct english pronunciation of the letter H (Protestant) or aspirated 'haych' (Catholic) – even your hairstyles. Some protestant girls from a flashpoint area of North Belfast we worked with, are able to tell a catholic girl from the positioning of the bobble for a pony tail – (it's high for a catholic and low for a protestant, in case you were wondering!) For a company working on both sides of the divide, it is essential to be aware of these symbols, and consequently acknowledge the restrictions they can place on our work. For instance if we are producing a play set in Northern Ireland, we want the children and young people to relate to it, and not be alienated because they read the symbols, and perceive it to be about people on the other side of the divide.

PHOTO: JILL JENNINGS

One Night in February

Our production of *Striking Distance*, by Raymond Scannell, is a classic case in point. This piece was originally performed by, and created for Graffiti Theatre, based in Cork in the South of Ireland. The play followed the story of a young guy who had moved with his mother from a big city, which we set as Belfast, to escape some violent trouble linked to his father, and start a new life for just the two of them. It explores a broad range of themes: emotional control, anger management, fitting in, peer pressure, repercussions of actions and suicide. In the original script the characters' names presented a problem. They were definitely Irish names, for example, Fergal and Aoife. In Northern Ireland only Catholics have traditional Irish, or biblical names. Being named after the Pope (like a friend of mine, John-Paul) is a real give away! So in order not to alienate anyone in the audience of *Striking Distance* the names were changed to Simon and Jess. The name of the school, St Marks had to be changed, as catholic schools are named after saints. It was also never stated where the mother and son had moved to, as certain towns, particularly the smaller rural ones, can be predominantly of one faith. People's perception of where the play was set, varied from community to community. Some setting it in a more republican area, and others a more unionist area.

Replay's Range of Themes

We are constantly trying to stretch the borders of what our audiences will accept, in an attempt to broaden their horizons, sometimes it is a case of what the teachers will accept. Some of the issue-based pieces the company has produced have evoked startling responses. For instance, *Yours Truly* by Marie Jones was developed in partnership with the Health Promotion Agency to highlight issues around teenage pregnancies. However the company soon discovered there were limits to what could be put in the play without offending numerous catholic, and stricter protestant schools. Pre-production discussions with teachers showed that no mention could be made of abortion or contraception – rather difficult in a play looking at teenage pregnancy. This blinkered attitude came across with other issue-based material, such as *Out of Their Heads*, a drugs piece by Marcus Romer ('our children don't do drugs'), or *Sinking* by Gary Mitchell a bullying piece ('there's no bullying in our school').

As well as issue-based pieces, Replay's productions and projects contain a richness and broad variety of styles. Some are designed to give young audiences a sense of pride about their heritage and a means of celebrating their common culture. Living histories (site specific pieces in historical sites of Northern Ireland). *Blood Lines* by

John McClelland (which showed the influence of the Vikings in Northern Ireland). *The Millies* by Nicola McCartney (the influence of the linen industry on Northern Ireland culture).

This highlighting of common ground between communities is so important in divided societies. It is a theme underlying much of our work, including shows with more universal themes, such as *You Choose* by Grant Corr (choices and decisions and their repercussions). Others like *Shalom Belfast* by Rebecca Bartlett (the impact of Jewish immigrants on Belfast's culture), or *Mirad a Boy from Bosnia* by Ad de Bont, are pushing people to look beyond their own conflict, to learn from others, to explore conflict one step removed through theatre as a safe medium, then to draw parallels, and realise that cultural baggage isn't always just about Catholics and Protestants.

Our workshop programme *Fortress Europe* in the format of a giant interactive board game developed to run in tandem with *Mirad*, focused on refugees and human rights, and proved so successful it ran as a stand-alone project for seven years, linking up with *Shalom Belfast*. When a spate of violence in the protestant Shankill area of Belfast saw people being displaced from their homes under threat of their lives, the workshop was suddenly directly mirroring what was happening in real life. It was too close to the bone for the community, and youth leaders cancelled the workshops.

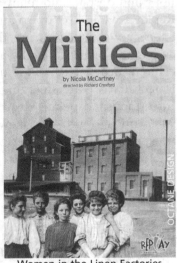

Women in the Linen Factories

Alongside the production of new commissions, existing plays and interactive work, the company has prioritised the need to develop local artists' and teachers' skills in using the arts to work with children and young people. So far, a masterclass series in working with nursery aged children, a six month writing project for young audiences – Script Lab culminated in the rehearsed reading of new scripts, and developed new writers. Currently, we are working with the local education authority's behavioural support team to explore the use of the arts in promoting good behaviour, a residency programme working with young people in pupil-referral units.

The Future

Replay has always strived to make its work relevant to its young audiences, constantly building bridges of understanding, respect and acceptance. The company has received awards for work in cultural diversity and community relations. But are we not all building bridges with our work for, and with children and young people? Through the arts they learn about and question the world around them, developing thoughts and opinions and discovering skills with which to face the life ahead.

Since 1968, when the violence of the current phase of 'The Troubles' erupted onto the streets, the people of Northern Ireland have been directly involved in communal conflict. Much violence, hope and despair and many political initiatives have followed. Since Replay was first set up so much has changed – the deserted evening streets now bustle with life, the check-points and searches have gone, as has the presence of the armed forces, and the now vibrant city centre is accessible at all hours. To live in Northern Ireland today, is to feel that we are emerging from the conflict which left more than three thousand people dead, and many thousands injured, that we stand on the brink of a new, peaceful, democratic, and potentially prosperous future. At the same time, there is a sure and certain knowledge, that there is also an almost equal chance of a catastrophic slide back into violence and chaos.

Let us hope that the inspirational work of arts organisations, working with children and young people, will never let that happen.

Richard Croxford worked with companies in the UK and Europe before becoming Director of Replay Productions in 2000.

2. INTERNATIONAL CONTEXT

WINDOW ON THE WORLD – ASSITEJ

Paul Harman outlines UK involvement in the development of ASSITEJ, and the gains and challenges of international contact.

Artists are unique. Like strong native trees, they are rooted in the soil of their own land. You cannot teach an apple tree to grow oranges. If we applied the images of trees and fruit to artists in a literal way, there would be no point in engaging with the arts of any community or culture other than one's own. While it may be hard to understand the cultural background which informs the way other people speak, paint or make theatre, the aims and techniques of human cultural and artistic expression are similar the world over. Both as artists and crafts-people making theatre, we need to learn from our peers – and we can.

The Formation of ASSITEJ

In the field of theatre for children and young people, one international network above all has provided a gateway to potential partners and sources of ideas. Many UK practitioners of the last forty years have benefited from contacts made through it. The International Association of Theatre for Children and Young People – known by its French acronym, ASSITEJ – had its founding meeting in London in 1965. Key UK theatre and drama specialists, including Peter Slade, had met US, Russian, Czech, and French fellow enthusiasts at meetings of the ITI (International Theatre Institute). Together, they decided that an organisation to focus attention on theatre for children, and provide a forum for artistic exchange should be formed. ITI had a relationship with UNESCO, and ASSITEJ was intended to be a 'third tier' organisation in relation to and hopefully supported by UNESCO. A number of such specialist bodies exist, such as UNIMA, for puppetry, and others for theatre critics, and designers.

One of the implicit aims of the founders of ASSITEJ and similar bodies was to provide a bridge across the Iron Curtain, to enable cultural links between artists in the two competing world systems of the time, which then appeared to be in a precarious balance. The founding articles of association refer to 'the interests of world peace'. Activity was based around a Congress every three years, held at a major international festival with productions from every continent. In practice, ASSITEJ has remained a quite small, voluntary body with little influence on policy at an international level. However, the very existence of ASSITEJ has enabled practitioners to make contact with colleagues overseas, to travel and develop exchanges, with government support or permission.

At each Congress, a General Assembly of the membership is held. Each National Centre has three votes, to represent professional and amateur theatre for children in the country. The membership elects an Executive Committee every three years. In the early years, a powerful Bureau was also elected, which effectively controlled policy. The organisation has been dependent on the goodwill and bounty of governments prepared to put up the money to house delegates, pay for a world festival, and provide translators for the formal meetings. The USA and USSR have done so twice. The UK has not hosted a Congress, but has always had a member on the Executive.

Early Leadership from the Soviet Bloc and France

In the early years of international ASSITEJ, the strong personalities of a number of women in key leadership positions determined the way things were carried on. Natalya Satz had been asked by Lenin to create theatre for children orphaned by the revolution and civil war. After being exiled by Stalin she fought her way back to influence and continued her mission. By the 1960's, the USSR had a world-class network of professional theatres for children in all its major cities. Ilse Rodenberg, widow of the first Minister of Culture of the German Democratic Republic, supported the development of similar formal theatre companies in many countries in the socialist bloc, including Cuba. Rosemarie Moudoues, the French General Secretary of ASSITEJ from its foundation until 1990, saw to it that the cultural influence, and strongly artist-led practice of the Latin countries of Europe, remained predominant.

ASSITEJ in the UK had been maintained by the original supporters of the international ideal, notably John English, founder of the visionary Midlands Arts Centre for Young People. In 1981, five younger workers in professional theatre for young people with a background in the Theatre-iniEducation (TIE) movement, crammed into a Ford Fiesta and drove to Lyons for an ASSITEJ congress. We became part of a new movement.

New Directions within ASSITEJ

Over the next ten years there was a fierce ideological battle within ASSITEJ between those who believed in theatre as a form descended from the Greek model, made by professionals for children to watch in formal theatre buildings – and those who saw the future in a broader range of activities, from participatory theatre in schools and 'theatre for development' by non-professionals in developing countries. In North-Western Europe, notably in Scandinavia and Germany, there had developed a theatre of empowerment for children characterised by collective and co-operative working, small-scale touring and a focus on children's feelings and personal needs. By 1990, at the Stockholm Congress, this battle came to a head, and a significant change in the direction and policy of ASSITEJ followed, under the leadership of the Scandinavian Centres, backed by generous subsidy from their governments. Since then, the membership of ASSITEJ has doubled to include many more countries in the developing world, whose approach to theatre is very different from the mainly European founding members.

The Language Issue

Since 2002, the UK has been represented by Jeremy Turner of Arad Goch Theatre in Wales, and theatre in minority communities and languages has risen up the international agenda. Paradoxically, a move to simplify exchange between members across the world, has led to the use of English as the working language. At the foundation of ASSITEJ, English, French and Russian were declared official languages, and at formal meetings translation had to be provided in all three, plus the language of the country in which the meeting was being held. This made it impossible to meet without great expense, and frequently produced a House of Babel effect where mistranslation of technical terms caused many misunderstandings. Very few of the members of the Executive Committee were multilingual in the early days. In recent years, younger professionals in most countries of the world are well educated in English, and direct communication is much easier.

Theatre Texts

In Eastern Europe there is a tradition of featuring international work within the repertoire of theatres for children. Few UK companies had produced plays from abroad as UK theatre had proven to be resistant to outside influences. Apart from Ibsen, Chekhov, Brecht and Anouilh – the UK adult theatre-goer rarely encountered a non-British voice which was not American.

Much theatre for children in the UK is made by a locally-based company. Regional social issues pertinent to the lives of their young audiences form the basis of new play commissions. Arts Council funding has encouraged writing aimed at particular audiences and specific age ranges. Companies which offer adaptations of well-known stories, or children's books are popular, but have not attracted public funding. As David Wood reports, theatre for parents and children in 'family time' is extensive, though probably not so much as in the USA.

PHOTO: PAT MAYCROFT

Paul Harman in '*Bedtime Stories*'

The main UK practice in the publicly-funded companies since the 60's, had been to focus on social themes of interest to teachers who book shows for children to watch in school time. This theatre had a key relevance to the educational, social and cognitive development of children – in contrast to many countries in ASSITEJ, where theatre is seen as an independent, artistic field contributing to children's cultural, emotional and spiritual development.

International contact and exchange

In the 70's and 80's Caryl Jenner and Nicholas Barter were keen supporters of internationalism at the Unicorn Theatre. Unicorn celebrated the building-based theatre style of Central and Eastern

Europe, and was the UK Centre of ASSITEJ. New plays by the younger generation of UK playwrights were complemented by work from the European 'theatre of empowerment', typified by Volker Ludwig's Grips Theater in West Berlin. Traffic began to flow both ways.

UK writer Roy Kift was commissioned by the German company, Grips, to write a play for the International Year of Disabled People in 1990. *Stronger than Superman* is a typical Grips play, in a lively cabaret style with fast pace and Brechtian musical breaks – 'to allow children to discuss the previous scene'. Several UK companies followed Unicorn's lead in producing Grips plays on racism, being in hospital and the need for city children to have places to play. In the course of the 1990's, several UK directors, such as Guy Holland of Quicksilver Theatre, worked abroad in countries with developed theatre traditions, like Russia and Japan, and their companies have toured widely. The creative partnerships which have developed from such encounters, originally made through ASSITEJ events world-wide, has contributed to a broader range of approaches now available to UK audiences.

At first, the best UK play texts for children and young people were only picked up in English-speaking countries, like Australia and Canada. More recently, UK plays have been recognised for their quality by producers in many more countries, largely as a result of contacts through ASSITEJ. Henning Fangauf reports on links to Germany.

The Challenge of International Contact

An informal survey in 2002, showed that by then some forty companies had had international exchanges, or tours during the previous five years. The ASSITEJ network had provided information about festivals around the world, at which many kinds of theatre production could be seen. It is rare now to find a UK artistic director who has not travelled abroad to see shows, or to take part in an exchange. However, while any artist continually absorbs new ideas, using such influences is not a straightforward process. The actors the director works with in the UK, and those he has seen overseas, may have been trained in quite different performing traditions.

I believe that the primary purpose of international cultural exchange and exposure to different traditions is to challenge one's own preconceptions.

At various times over the last thirty years I have been greatly inspired by wonderful performances and productions by children's theatre companies from around the world.

- Leningrad director and guru of a generation of Russian theatre makers, Korogodsky's production of *Bambi*, in which actors in simple modern pullovers, arms raised above their heads, told the moving story of a herd of deer which brought tears to the eyes, even if you did not understand the text.
- Adolph Shapiro's company from Riga, Latvia, presented stirring and challenging productions full of detail and focused energy.
- Kaze-no-ko Company from Japan told stories about the pressure on contemporary children through traditional fables delivered in stunningly choreographed pictures.
- From Belgium, the members of Théâtre de la Galafronie, in a repertoire of surrealist shows over twenty years, like *Le Piano Sauvage*, touch feelings buried deep below the surface of our conscious understanding.
- Suzanne Osten at Unga Klara in Stockholm, has likewise addressed the personal feelings and concerns young people have about the behaviour of the adults around them, through immaculately composed stories about divorce, adult passion and madness.

ASSITEJ has provided me and many of my contemporaries with a constant flow of possibilities for new contacts and experiences. I have watched plays alongside the children of fifty countries. Every encounter adds a little to my understanding of the art and craft of making theatre for children.

Paul Harman is Artistic Director of Cleveland Theatre Company who produce the Take-off Festival. He is Chair of the ASSITEJ UK Board.

OPENING DOORS WITH EASTERN EUROPE

Sarah Kettlewell describes how Playtime Theatre has set up links and practical exchanges with children's theatre companies in Eastern Europe.

Playtime Theatre Company

We were established in 1983 with the aim of taking innovative and imaginative theatre to children and young people in Kent but we quickly grew, extending our touring area to include the whole of south-east England. Now, we tour work nationally – and internationally. We are based in the coastal town of Whitstable, in Kent, a short hop across the English Channel.

We produce between one to three new plays per year, and give in the region of two hundred performances, in schools, theatres, and arts centres, youth clubs and at festivals. Topics are wide-ranging – everything from fairy tales to local history stories, to Chaucer. All (with one exception) are company-devised, and we also run drama workshops. Most of our plays are highly visual, and include audience participation – in some productions, the children even determine the ending of the plays! All our plays have a strong narrative and wherever possible, incorporate a variety of different art forms, including puppetry, mime, physical theatre, music and song.

Cross-cultural Links

In 1993, as part of a growing interest in forging cross-cultural links with Europe and situated so close to continental Europe (Dover is but twenty miles away), we saw the opportunity and challenge that touring abroad might give us. As a consequence, Playtime commenced a programme of European touring and 'reciprocal exchanges' with other children's theatre companies in Europe. The basis of these 'exchanges' is that Playtime organises a tour in the UK for the foreign company, taking care of all the bookings, accommodation, travel arrangements, press and publicity, then the visiting company arranges a tour in their country for Playtime, taking care of all the arrangements at their end. In this way, all the 'hard slog' usually associated with touring abroad was avoided, with both companies being able to utilize their local knowledge of everything from venues through to accommodation.

It had been our original plan to try and set up an exchange with either a Dutch or French company, not least because of their geographical proximity. However, with a large part of our repertoire being aimed at the primary school age range, we perceived problems with the language barrier in these countries. We therefore began to look further afield. We had a Hungarian fundraiser at the time, and our first exchange was with a children's theatre company from Hungary.

How we set up Exchanges

Our initial visit provided an opportunity to view, at first hand (rather than on video), the different companies' work. The most important factor was to find a company which shared our artistic vision, and would work in a similar way to us. One has to bear in mind that at this point in time, in 1992, Hungary was just emerging from Communist rule, where theatre had been extremely well-funded, where every major city had its own dedicated children's theatre. Playtime was a touring company with three staff, no core funding, without a theatre building, performing 90% of its work in schools. Our partners therefore had to be able to work under these limitations. By the same token, Playtime's plays would not have been suitable for the large-scale Hungarian State Theatres with over 2000 seats!

In 1993, we began our relationship with Kolibri Szinhaz, a new young company – themselves only established in 1992 – whose artistic director didn't speak a word of English and had relatively little experience of touring! It was an amazing leap of faith on the part of both artistic directors, but truly visionary. It proved incredibly successful, and opened up new vistas for both of us. Kolibri Szinhaz have toured England for ten consecutive years, returning to tour theatres and schools, and for the Canterbury Festival. I should add that they have gone on to become one of the most highly regarded children's theatre companies in Europe. They now have a permanent company of over twenty actors and give in the region of 450 to 500 performances per year. Although originally for children, their repertoire nowadays regularly features plays for adults too (including *Monty Python and the Holy Grail!*)

Buoyed by this initial success, the following year we embarked on setting up a similar exchange with a company from the Czech Republic. We approached, and are indebted to the ASSITEJ staff in Prague. They made contact with theatre companies which proved to be invaluable. We went ahead with Theater Minor, their oldest children's theatre company. Their director did speak a little English. Again, the exchange proved to be a huge success. Other exchanges have taken place with companies from Portugal, Germany and Slovakia.

Language Barriers

One of the first questions people are always keen to ask about is 'the language barrier'. In this respect, it has been rather easier for Playtime, when we tour our work abroad, as all the companies with whom we have worked have been keen to have a production in the English language. Indeed, it is one of the overriding reasons for collaborating

The performance is about to begin

with an English company. Because Playtime's productions tend to be highly visual, and the children have some comprehension of the English language, our plays have worked well. Since audience participation is vital to the execution of our plays, the key points of the storyline are always translated, and we perform in the local language.

When I said that Playtime has had it 'easier' than its foreign counterparts, in terms of language, this is because English schools and theatres do not share the same enthusiasm or need, for a play performed in a foreign language, so the visiting companies perform in English. Because much of our work is performed in schools, it has been easy for us to prepare the audiences well in advance with accompanying notes for children and teachers, not only about the play, but also to tell them about the country the company come from, and introduce a few words of the language. One of the best welcomes a foreign company ever received was from a small village school in Kent, where the whole school had learnt a welcome in Hungarian and Hungarian flags were flying in the school hall! This was a theatrical experience for the school, but a cultural exchange as well.

The Benefits

From Playtime's point of view, touring abroad has brought a new dimension to our work, opened up new opportunities for us and enabled us to develop as an organisation. On collaborative productions, it has encouraged the free flow of ideas and expertise between theatre practitioners, writers and designers and has given us an insight into a variety of different cultures, backgrounds and theatre traditions. Our creativity has been enhanced by such work and we have learnt new skills. Above all, it has been fun! From our young audiences' point of view, the benefits have been innumerable; exposure to different cultures and ideas; widening and developing experience and imagination; encouraging cross-cultural understanding and co-operation, to name but three.

From our initial ideas behind the 'exchanges', other projects and partnerships have developed, particularly in Hungary. One of the most successful of these has been with a company called Ringlispil, run by the well-known actress and director, Kovats Kriszta. Ringlispil have toured the UK on four occasions with *Over the Seasons* – such has been the demand. Playtime and Ringlispil will collaborate on a new version of Lewis Carroll's *Alice in Wonderland*; the cast to include both Hungarian and English actors.

One of the most extraordinary ventures to come about from the exchange programme was when Kolibri Szinhaz decided to translate one of Playtime Theatre's plays – *Jeremy Snow* – and include it in their repertoire. Nothing particularly amazing about that you might think, until you know that they asked if they might tour their version of the play in the UK, in English! Nick Champion, Playtime's director, was asked to correct their text. For the play's premiere in Hungary, Playtime presented their version in the same venue that Kolibri presented their adaptation, an awe-inspiring experience. *Jeremy Snow* has since been adapted for Hungarian TV, and is a set text on a university drama course.

This is not to say that the exchange programme has been without its hiccups. The potential for things to go wrong on a venture of this scale are enormous – the wrong technician on the work permit, declined entry at Dover, props and scenery impounded at Heathrow, delay on the Austrian-Hungarian border due to Carnet problems with a performance looming at nine o'clock the next morning, to name but a few. Thank heaven for the European Union! However, the long-term benefits and experience derived from working with foreign companies, together with the excitement and impetus it can give one's company cannot be emphasised enough – they far exceed any downside.

Go on – try it for yourselves. You won't be disappointed!

Sarah Kettlewell is Administrator of Playtime Theatre.

AN OUTSIDE EYE – UK Writers Performed in the Repertoire in Germany

Germany supports an extensive network of state-funded professional companies with a big demand for new playtexts. Henning Fangauf reports on the development in the repertoire of plays by UK writers Translation by Paul Harman.

The First Stones flew in 1967

Peter Stein staged Edward Bond's *Saved* in Munich. One scene in particular shocked the audience: a group of young people, out of sheer boredom, stoned a baby in a pram and killed it. This barbarity against an innocent being seemed to break a taboo and Bond's play left deep wounds. His apparently naturalistic play did not only open a window on the inner life of a working-class area of London, but defined the image of British drama in Germany for the years that followed.

It was Peter Stein again who did the first German production of Nigel William's *Class Enemy*. The play was explicitly intended for 'teenagers, parents and teachers'. A class, having driven out their teacher, is waiting for something to happen and passes the time in continual (self)-destruction. Boredom drives them to aggression. Apparent play turns into a fight for existence. The production marked a milestone in the development of German theatre for young people, however contentious. The question was how the feelings of young people should be represented. Peter Stein's choreographic production was criticised. 'That's Broadway, New York, not Kreuzberg, Berlin ... It's entertainment for everybody' wrote the trade journal *Theater Heute* in June 1981.

With this play a certain opinion about British contemporary drama became fixed in the minds of critics and theatre buffs: as hard-edged, utterly realistic, taboo-breaking theatre, which took its themes and characters from "lower class" streets of big cities. More and more German producers were interested in these plays.

Family entertainment

In contrast also from Britain came West End style entertainment, played pre-dominantly on the main stages of German City Theatres. Their Christmas programmes featured not only Grimm and other fairy tales but also English stories. AA Milne's classic *Pooh Bear*, appeared regularly on the big stages, with Dickens' *Christmas Carol*. Alan Ayckbourn was popular with *Mr A's Amazing Plays*.

David Wood. *The Gingerbread Man* alone had over one hundred German productions. Children loved to dream with him and the characters on the kitchen dresser. Still played today are *The Ideal Gnome Expedition* and *Plotters of Cabbage Patch Corner*. All these plays are written as light entertainment, they have music and are intended for the larger stage. They offer many possibilities for directors and designers and they encourage children to join in robustly.

Plays for the Times

In the 80's realistic British plays, Barrie Keefe's *Barbarians* and *Gimme Shelter*, Trevor Griffiths' *Skins*, Phil Young's *Kissing God*, and Willy Russell's *Blood Brothers* conquered the German repertoire. A great service to this transfer was contributed by the Bremen literary agency LITAG under its manager and translator, Angela Kingsford Röhl. Her agency handled the rights to plays by over twenty contemporary British authors of theatre for children and young people.

The underbelly of British everyday life was shown in hard realism. British drama, unlike any other in Europe, looks at the losers in society and Germany, since the Reunification of 1990, can identify with that. Directors and actors found that the content and the drawing of characters made new demands, and opened up discussion about realism on stage. The plays brush no problems aside, and no easy laughs or well-crafted discussions are allowed.

JAK young people's theatre in Hamburg, directed by Jurgen Zielinski, used the special ambience of their performing space, a disused factory, for an impressive production of Griffiths' *Skins*. In a Manchester warehouse a Skinhead Band rehearses for a gig. They have the chance to play in a big concert. But there's a catch: it's a promotional event for the Far Right. The no holds barred argument about whether it is possible to distance oneself as an artist from political ideology threatens to split the group. Zielinski's production was depressingly violent, was much characterised as "highly authentic" and invited to the 1993 Berlin Festival as "one of the most noteworthy productions of the season".

Philip Ridley. *Sparkleshank* was performed at the annual Writer's Forum in Frankfurt. In an interview, he said of his writing that it was fundamentally autobiographical. 'I have always written about things I know: London's East End, the beaten up urban landscape. That gives my writing a truth based in reality.' Jake, the lead character in *Sparkleshank*, is an outsider who cannot come to terms with the violent rituals of his class. He uses another weapon, namely language – with this he gains respect and can build relationships with his classmates. The play has a fairy tale ending. 'If you think about the old folk tales, the stories happen in dirty little villages, where we would set them in a slum. I use these set pieces of the traditional folk-tale in a modern setting.'

It evolved within the framework of BT Connections 1996 organised by the Royal National Theatre. Along with twelve other writers, Ridley was asked to write a play for Youth Theatre actors, not professionals. The play has been successful in many Youth Theatre Clubs attached to German City Theatres. In all Ridley's plays one basic theme is addressed: what chance do children and young people have to escape from their social circumstances and build a unique and better life for themselves? Ridley leads his characters into the worlds of magic and dreams.

Simon Stephens. He also addresses this theme too, but comes to a more open-ended conclusion. *Herons* deals with a teenager, Billy, who is the victim of bullying. Billy's weak and incompetent father has informed on a relative of his chief tormentor and after suffering a severe assault, Billy only turns the tables by threatening the gang with a gun. The location of the play is a lonely stretch of polluted urban canal. In Stephen's metaphor-rich text, he suggests that Herons can always fly away. Simon Stephens' works with the Young Writers Programme at the Royal Court Theatre, London. His plays are often played in Germany by a combination of professional actors and young actors from youth theatre clubs.

Children's Theatre

Use of British plays for younger audiences only started in Germany in the mid-90's. For too long an idea had prevailed that these plays were less dramatic literature than outlines for Theatre-in-Education programmes. But once again certain individuals discovered interesting authors and their plays, got them translated and taken up by agencies. Three examples illustrate the trend.

Charles Way made a name for himself in Germany with an adaptation of Homer's *Odyssey*. Way tells the old story from the perspective of Odysseus' son, Telemachus. The play questions the role of the father in the family, in society and our expectations of the role. Telemachus is disillusioned because his father does not return as a conquering hero. Charles Way talks about love and nature, myths and traditions. He does not write for the mainstream but for him theatre is 'a place for community and a place of hope.'

Mike Kenny. *Song from the Sea* and *Walking the Tightrope*, are convincing not only for their poetic language but because they bring together different generations in interesting ways. Grandmother and Grandfather are always the ones who determine the course of the action. Their experience of life is contrasted with the aspirations of their grandchildren. This special personality and the dialogue between the generations make Kenny's plays so valuable and unique.

Nick Wood. Warrior Square (translated into German as *Fluchtwege – Escape Routes* – won the prestigious Berlin Brothers Grimm Prize in 2003. Two refugee children from Bosnia come to terms with life in a hostile English seaside town. The play sides with children who suffer most from the consequences of hatred and prejudice. It is also a parable. With strong determination, children in such circumstances can take their lives into their own hands and overcome hatred and prejudice. Thalia Theater, Hamburg commissioned him to write a play for the classroom. The resulting play *Mia* had a double premiere in Hamburg and at Nottingham Playhouse in 2005.

In the repertoire

Interest in British plays for children and young people has grown steadily over the last twenty-five years, and since 2000 there has been a strong swell of success. British drama has freed itself from the view that it was all realistic, issue-based theatre. Current plays from Britain are enriching our repertoire with clear, well-told stories, drawing their subject matter from Antiquity to the Present, characters have a fully rounded psychology, there's a richness of metaphor and emotional expression. New plays are awaited expectantly and German companies are looking for collaborations with British authors.

Henning Fangauf is Deputy Director of the National Development Centre for Theatre for Children and Young People, in Frankfurt, Germany, with responsibility for international exchange and new writing development.

THEATRE FOR YOUNG PEOPLE IN THE THIRD WORLD
– Cultural Action as Social Transformation

David Pammenter outlines the theory and practice of Theatre-In-Education/Forum Theatre/and Theatre For Development, and describes a project with Street Children in Zambia.

Theatre as an artistic medium for communicating human experience, and theatre as an educational and social force are in reality pursuing the same objectives. The making of meaning in pursuit of change, human development and cultural transformation are the purposes and potential of both forms. Both are to do with the way we perceive the world, and the way we perceive ourselves and others. This holds true whether we are observing the art produced, or whether we are constructing it. Both are utterly dependent on the practice of communication, and the cultural realities in which communication occurs.

I want to explore commonalities between Theatre-in-Education, and Theatre for Development, and what they offer in the contemporary context. They are forms of action central to the cultural and political transformations demanded by the contemporary context.

Asking Questions Internationally

TIE was the product of a world full of questions. Why is the world as it is? What is determining our place in the dominant social order? Who controls the means of communication, and in whose interest? These questions were being asked in many countries, and by many people. Radical pedagogies began to be formulated and tested related to the United Nations, the Declaration of Human Rights (1948) and the Convention on the Rights of the Child (1989). In a globalised world, the impulse today towards transformation is growing ever stronger among the marginalised and unrepresented. More informed dialogue emerges about the realities of many parts of the world. The problems and historical realities of Africa, Asia and Latin America for which we were once content to shed a tear but do little or nothing about, are now increasingly seen as our problems too.

Against this background, we can see the impulse for change which was the driving force for the development of TIE and Theatre for Development and which grows even more strongly now. Not as a fanciful 'good' idea, but as a prerequisite part of the process of renaming our world so that we can determine for ourselves what our individual and collective lives, cultures and realities will be. That requires each of us to put ourselves at the centre of our own stories, and to encourage others to do the same. In early TIE – as David Holman relates – much of the form and content of our participatory theatre was concerned with the connection of 'self' with 'other'. We wanted to make the real world accessible for the children. We chose to tell the stories of other people in other times and other places, but from our real world in order that the child could discover more of what the world was, where it was and why it was. These stories, participatory or not in terms of performance, were about reflecting realities – and asking questions.

Pedagogy as a Tool

Artists, educators, theorists and community activists have long been aware of the need to forge a humanising curriculum which places the making of the people's world in the hands of the people themselves. For educational practitioners internationally, like Paolo Freire, Vygotski and Illich, pedagogy has been a tool for how trans-formation occurs. How do people learn? What is the content of their learning? Who determines the answers to these questions? Is educat-ion the means by which teachers fit students into the dominant culture – or a means by which they challenge it? Are the needs determined by the learner or the teacher?

What communication contains and how it occurs is crucial in terms of both the context and process of education. The way a social group sees itself, the way it sees and places its held ideas, its values, ethics, rights and responsibilities, is embedded in its systems of education.

Theatre for Development in Action

So let me tell you of my experience of co-creating a cultural action event in Zambia – a project concerned with Street Children. The project took place in the north of the country in a town called Mulifira with the small NGO (non government organisation) called *Safe T Child*.

The Street Children

The children were aged between six and thirteen. They were all occupying a place at the bottom of the hierarchy, which impacted heavily on their self-perception. Many of the stories, which emerged from their articulation, their drawing, and sharing of their life maps, were about feelings evoked by being at the base of the social pyramid in the family (where they were still in one) and on the street where they were not. Their collective experience, which became the source of the theatre they made, was of living in the context of everyone doing them a favour. They felt obliged to accept their whole existence because of the 'goodness' of somebody else – a cousin, an uncle, an NGO worker etc.

As a result, they are continually operating in response to coercion or oppression. In the family, which had taken them in after the loss of their parents, they felt they had to demonstrate their gratitude and accept their place in relation to the family group. They felt they were obliged to pray, and to thank God and their benefactors for their survival. In their view, the tasks of gathering the wood, doing the carrying, cleaning the yard, doing the washing, fell to them. They were the last to eat. They felt they had to acknowledge their status being placed below the 'real' children of the family in terms of respect, acceptance or even recognition. Many felt they were abused in this role physically, psychologically, and sometimes sexually. Some children had run away – and become Street Children to avoid this bond slavery.

The Workshop Process

The workshop is conducted with twenty children and was scheduled for one week. We start with introductory ice-breakers and relationship building. Then we begin to facilitate the articulation of their individual stories, and identify communal experiences. What is held in common? What do you recognise? What made you happy? What made you unhappy? Did you speak about it? Did you confront the people or the problem? Could you? Why? Why not? What do the others in this story need to think about? What do you think they need to do? The workshops are based on the needs of the children to find and articulate their collective voice. They unveil their collective realities and construct ways of enabling others to confront it.

They explore the creation of key still images, of tableaux, of moving sculptures, of music, movement, dance, the key moments of change, and turning points in their individual lives. Then the identification of the key underpinning issues and perceptions which collectively oppressed them. The children take the decisions in relation to what their collective voice will say.

The Role of Facilitator

My role is workshop facilitator. I'm working with three NGO activists from *Safe T Child*, one of whom is a local carpenter. Our job is the posing of questions, and the extension of the children's understanding of communication forms. When to stop the action with a still image for the audience to reflect? How to sharpen the audience's perception? What do we want the audience as participants to feel and think? Is our view a true reflection of reality? Where to give them the opportunity to question themselves?

These are the same kind of questions which a theatre writer asks in the construction of theatre. Through their pressing need to change both their own situation and the perception of them by others, we began to create the educational dialogues of which Paolo Freire speaks. We resisted the silencing imposed by our acquiesence to the orthodoxies of the powerful. We were not preoccupied with theatre understandings or skills. We were concerned with an inner reality and a process of collective creativity and action in terms of creating change in ourselves and change in others.

The Performances

These take place on a patch of land by the side of a road in front of the base of *Safe T Child*, which the children decorate with painted cloths, tables and chairs. As people arrive, the children greet them with songs of welcome, and move among their guests introducing themselves, shaking hands, and telling them what the event will be about. They then perform their song of introduction. There are four plays, lasting ten to twenty minutes. They are presentations of the journeys which comprise the lived experiences of the children. The characters wear simple costume, and perform using humour and a real sense of fun.

Much of the performance is improvised, rather than scripted, and all pieces are punctuated with movement, picture building and song.

The pieces use indigenously identifiable cultural roles, images, contexts and situations for easy recognition. Local songs and music with percussion and dance. The pieces illustrate the death of parents, the break up of the family, and the journey which followed. They present the complexities around the kinds of abuse the children received at the hands of extended family members, or carers. Some sections are naturalistic story journeys of the group of travelling children finding food, stealing, escaping police or people in local communities. The pieces change performance style from still image to moving sculpture, direct address to naturalism.

Forum Theatre

At some stage each play invites audience participation. Some are simple narratives based on the story of a central character with key turning points. Two of the pieces use 'frozen moments', and the questioning by the audience of the character decisions within the depiction. A child asks for audience suggestions for other ways of dealing with the problem. Members of the audience are invited to replace the child actor, and show how they think resolution could be found. Forum Theatre with the Street Child as the Facilitator.

The Audience Response

In one piece, the plot leads to the death of a child running away after violent and sexual abuse from her guardian. After her death from hunger and illness, her friends seek to bury her but they are chased away as trouble-makers by the local community. As she was someone they cared for, what are they to do? The Facilitator seeks advice from the audience, to test an improvised scene. The audience solution fails the Street Children. They feel it is based on other people being 'nice' to them. They perform their own real solution. This play came from a true story and provoked a lot of reflective debate with the audience. In all the pieces the children depicted their view of the realities, which led them into having to find solutions to problems in ways which they were not supposed to, or were not allowed by the communities. Within the dominant orthodoxies, the children's courses of action were frowned upon – or seen as criminal.

The performances had been powerful and disturbing. The audience had listened to things which they had ignored or set aside.

Listening provoked dialogue between the children, and their participatory audience. After the performances, the children brought food and drink for the audience, moving amongst them and entering into informal discussion. The children were the hosts and spoke with the adult and child guests as equals. The event raised the question which the children had intended – What is to be done? The Street Children and the audience began a collective process of seeking solutions, and answering the children's question, which was now their question too. This was the begin-ning of the action of social transformation.

"Before I couldn't face people
Now I can stand up"
Royce, performer with the disabled group

The project drew on the techniques developed in Theatre-in-Education. and Forum Theatre to create Theatre for Development.

Cultural Action as Social Transformation

The need is for social transformation – ending the silencing, developing rights in constructing our own futures. It is about understanding, evaluating and rejecting the control of the dominant. It is about re-examining our reality, trusting our capacity to reconstruct. Such work enables us to place a value on ourselves and others, and gain clarity in our collective purpose. It is about understanding and changing reality. An SS Officer visiting Picasso's studio in occupied Paris indicated a photo of Guernica with the question, 'Did you do this?' Picasso's response was, 'No, you did!' The historic impact of the painting has been enormous. It has prevented the silencing of history. Brecht said; 'only taught by reality, can reality be changed.'

When orphaned children in Indonesia are helped to draw pictures of their experience of the Tsunami by teachers, artists and by NGO workers, an articulation is being achieved which enables distance and reflection. When Brecht articulated his major pedagogy, and generated a transformation in our understandings and capacities in the making of theatre for transformation, he was doing a similar thing. When our National Theatre performs David Hare's play *Stuff*

Happens, questioning the Blair-Bush role in the war in Iraq, a disturbance occurs for us as audience, which we must make sense of. The work in Zambia was a disturbance for all who participated, which we must make sense of, and move forward into action.

TIE began in a period of social change and was a search for transformation. Forum Theatre was developed in the oppressed areas of Brazil as a method of involving the audience in change. The wheel of history brings us again to a period of global social change. Today, in finding and giving our voice and asserting our identities in the building of our own futures, we are participants in the action of social transformation. We have to confront the question posed by the Street Children of Zambia and make, with them and others, a practical response in the concrete form of action. What is to be done? How and when are we going to do it?

David Pammenter was an active member of the TIE movement. He now devises and delivers programmes in Theatre for Development at University College Winchester.

3. BUILDING-BASED THEATRE

UNICORN – THE PIONEER CHILDREN'S THEATRE

Why has it taken fifty years to achieve funding for what some countries have always had – a dedicated theatre building for children? Tony Graham gives an account of the Unicorn's achievements throughout this period.

The Unicorn was the first children's theatre company to gain national recognition. A closer look at the Unicorn's fifty year history tells a story – about arts and education funding in Britain – and about dedication to high quality theatre for children.

Taking Theatre to the People

In 1947, a Mobile Theatre was formed as an offshoot of Amersham Playhouse in Buckinghamshire. The director was Caryl Jenner who had worked in many branches and styles of theatre. With other radicals like Joan Littlewood and the Theatre Workshop, she was driven by the zeal that was knocking down a class-ridden social order. Middle-class taste was not only dominant, but also largely stagnant. West End audiences watched actors in dinner jackets and fashionable attire performing plays that rarely offered more perspective than that seen through a French window. If the people did not come to the theatre, theatre had to be taken to the people.

Caryl Jenner decided on a new course of action. The company took to the road. As part of the new venture she formed the Unicorn Theatre – for children between five and twelve, sending out three touring companies to play venues across Britain.

Playwriting for Children

Jenner's fierce standards are evident in her thoughts on writing plays for children. So many adults underestimate a child's powers of comprehension and make it too simple. Many of the play manuscripts which are rejected fall into this trap. It takes a very perceptive person to get inside the mind of a child and know what will work. For Jenner, taking theatre to the people, especially young people, was not enough.

She was also conscious of the need for new material and new ways of playing. Jenner knew that children, above all, would respond more readily to a truthful theatre.

How to act for Children?

Again she set a high standard. According to Stanislavsky: 'as for adults, only better.' She was well aware of the stigma attached to 'a kid's play', and this treasured quote was an important weapon in her armoury.

In a booklet issued to new company members, actors were given these instructions:

> "Great imaginative ability is required to attain belief in the fantastic characters and situations found in infant plays, and this is essential if you are to play them with conviction in a technique which demands frequent direct contact with the audience, as well as fellow actors. Absolute care must be taken when first approaching these plays in rehearsal not to fall into the trap of 'talking down' to the children. The actor must see through the children's eyes, and play with the directness and simplicity that he would find from the child itself."

National Funding Policies

In 1961, the Arts Council claimed that adult theatre was their remit, theatre for children should be the responsibility of the Ministry of Education, which in turn allocated responsibility to local education authorities. This throws some light on the lack of a strategic policy for state funding for children's theatre.

Jenner: 'It makes me blind with rage when I think that Yugoslavia has 123 state-subsidised children's theatres, the Soviet Union 300.' America had even more (though not professional). The Ministry of Education favoured local education authority support for children's theatre companies, rather than seeing it as a national strategic goal. The Arts Council only gradually came to accept the importance of funding theatre for children nationally. This has undermined its national development, and been responsible for imbalanced regional funding and insufficient national funding. Theatre for children and young people in the UK was not recognised as being of national significance, and therefore worthy of receiving regular state revenue.

Then, Jennie Lee, the first Minister of Culture, in Harold Wilson's 1964 Labour Party government, gave the first commitment to a National Theatre – though it did not open on the South Bank until 1976. She also introduced a synthesising approach to the arts, seeing them as integral to the development and good of the whole community. According to Lee: 'The opportunity to enjoy art has been mostly restricted to people with money and leisure, and I believe it is one of the duties of a socialist government to change that. If we make the best in the arts available to our children they will respond. Children are like sponges. They soak everything up.'

Theatre for Children comes to the West End

Finally, after a major campaign, the Arts Council agreed to provide a regular subsidy to support the work of the Unicorn. In 1967, Jenner was able to announce the first permanent base for her company at the Arts Theatre in the West End, London's theatreland. From now on, the company were able to perform weekdays as well as weekends and holidays. The auditorium was altered to allow children seated in the Circle to see the stage more clearly and the Box Office counter was lowered so that children could see the staff selling tickets. Jenner: 'the Unicorn only exists because you believe in it.' Years of subsistence theatre, touring on meagre wages, negotiating for funds, struggling with reluctant vans, out-of-date equipment, cold venues, colder digs, Jenner had been driven by an unswerving belief – now the Unicorn Theatre did exist!

Ten years later, Polka Theatre, a touring children's company, established its base in South London. They were the only building-based companies in Britain devoted to children's theatre.

Funding for School Groups

Theatre visits in London were subsidised by the Inner London Education Authority (ILEA) which developed comprehensive support for drama and theatre provision and practice. Under the leadership of Drama Inspectors, the ILEA had become one of the major centres of school drama development. It supported centres of educational theatre for young people (The Cockpit, The Curtain, Greenwich Young People's Theatre). The ILEA subsidised school visits to the Unicorn and the Polka Theatres, and enabled access via its cross-borough fleet of school buses. Such a positive approach to the theatre helped to create a pro-arts atmosphere which permeated all London schools. It also legitimised the work of drama teachers, whose own professional network grew during this period, while creating a bridge between the world of education and the world of professional theatre.

However, from the mid-1960's TIE and socially-aware theatre began to occupy centre stage, and a rift began. Children's theatre was seen as safe, apolitical and lacking in vision. Whereas Jenner had once been in the vanguard of social change, the Unicorn was now seen by some to have lagged behind, and to have immunised itself against the 60's revolution. How true was this? A closer look at the writers commissioned, their subject matter, the approach to making theatre, and casting policies reveals a highly enlightened, independent artistic leadership at the Unicorn. This new period had opened up as, tragically, Caryl Jenner died in 1973 at the age of fifty-five. Her extraordinary dedication had led her to work an eighteen hour day, fifty weeks of the year, with no assistant.

The Unicorn and New Writing

Matyelok Gibbs took over as Artistic Director. She was then working with the successful writer and director, Alan Ayckbourn, but came back because it looked as though the company was going to die with its founder. Gibbs believed that it was the function of her theatre to provide the audience with a broad range of good plays that were relevant to young people's concerns. In the early 70's, children had little influence and few rights. Gibbs felt that this was something that the Unicorn should address. Her plans for the new building exemplified her philosophy that children should feel and be in control of their decision-making – from whether to buy an ice cream, to what they thought about the play.

In 1977, Gibbs handed the baton over to Nicholas Barter, who had experience with the Arts Council Drama Department. The Barter era (1977 to 1986) can be characterised by an innovative approach to new writing. Barter was able to draw on a much wider writing milieu than ever before. He staged new plays and adaptations by established children's playwright David Wood, who became 'the national playwright for children', like *Meg and Mog*, a highly popular show. At the same time, socially-conscious drama was being presented. *Stronger Than Superman* by Roy Kift, produced in 1981, is about a ten year old with spina bifida who overcomes prejudice and patronising attitudes through a cheerful inability to accept the label of 'a child in a wheelchair'. Kift's plays were discovered through the work of Grips, Volker Ludwig's celebrated pioneering German theatre company for children, whose refreshing attitudes to theatre for children overturned many preconceptions about content, casting and form.

Another playwright produced was Dennis Foon, who founded Green Thumb Theatre in Vancouver in 1975. Green Thumb's mandate was to create original Canadian plays based on contemporary social issues which are of concern to young audiences. Its mission was 'to enlighten and empower young people by providing accessible, relevant, emotionally-grounded insights into young people's issues – without preaching, proselytising or condescension... and encouraging critical thinking and debate.' (Green Thumb Manifesto)

The ethos of this company was one that permeated many companies now working for young people. It was a philosophy that Barter adopted for the Unicorn. One of Barter's achievements was to transform the social and political into all areas of the Unicorn's work. Here's Barter on casting of an African folk tale: '*Anansi* is the first production where the cast is more black than white, but we have had integrated casting, not necessarily in Afro-Asian roles, for years now.' The Unicorn was also one of the first companies to have sign-interpreted performances for deaf and hearing-impaired children.

Funding under the Tories

Two new artistic directors, Chris Wallis in 1986 and Richard Williams from 1990, continued the commitment to high quality writing, but had to contend with the draconian policies of the Tory monetarists which were disastrous for those working in this sector. The Labour-led ILEA, which had been a key factor in the Unicorn's success, was axed by Thatcher along with its Labour-controlled political parent, the Greater London Council. Subsidy in the form of coaches, reduced ticket prices and advisory support was now a thing of the past. Whereas adult theatre was able to increase ticket prices, this was not an option for a children's theatre.

The Unicorn leaves the Arts Theatre

It was proving harder to attract new audiences, especially children, to the West End. Central London was perceived to be a less safe place. Day-time traffic had turned the West End into a gridlocked network. In 1997, when I took over as Director, closure seemed to be an inevitable destiny for the Unicorn which was in financial deficit. The company was given eight months to wind up its operations unless the deficit could be overturned and the building issues addressed. After a few years of struggling, we decided to move the Unicorn out of the Arts Theatre, and make a final stand over a new theatre building dedicated to children. The company was restructured to include an Education Department which would forge its own creative pro-grammes alongside, but independ-

PHOTO: PATRICK BALDWIN

Philip Pullman's *Clockwork*

ently of the artistic programme. The Unicorn moved to a base in North London.

The loss of the Arts Theatre encouraged the company to build new partnerships with exciting venues and companies, including co-productions with acclaimed companies like storytelling Theatre rites, and the disability company, Graeae. A series of artistic successes has followed including the TMA Children's Award for Best Production 2001 for *Tom's Midnight Garden* (which toured to the New Victory, New York), the critically-acclaimed dance-drama *Red Red Shoes* (awarded the Arts Council's annual Children's Writing Award in 2004) and international touring to Singapore with Adrian Mitchell's adaptation of the Beatrix Potter stories *Jemima Puddle Duck and Her Friends*.

In 2004, we broke new ground with an original opera for children based on Philip Pullman's novella *Clockwork*. This finished its tour with a residency at the Linbury Studio, Royal Opera House, to considerable acclaim from audiences, theatre and opera critics alike.

The New Unicorn

After sustained fundraising and restrucuring the Unicorn has, after fifty years, found a site and secured funding in central London for a dedicated children's theatre building to open in 2005. The Arts Council England, which has strategically backed the new enterprise through its Lottery Programme with a £5 million capital grant, has also increased the Unicorn's existing revenue funding in order to allow the company to achieve its ambitious goals. It is yet another key moment in the life of the Unicorn to build on the work of the pioneers while transcending our preconceptions.

Today, the company is focused and stable, and is able to concentrate on producing an innovative programme that offers both contemporary theatre for children, and an imaginative participatory/ educational practice. Our preoccupation at the Unicorn revolves around the issue of creating quality theatre for children. Deriving practices from European models, I hope to produce less work over a longer period of time, rather than ending up on a factory treadmill that churns out more work with ever-decreasing value.

Adrian Mitchell, radical poet and one-time writer in residence at the Unicorn, has argued that if every town can have a football team, it should also house a children's theatre. Whether or not the Unicorn is able to realise and sustain Caryl Jenner's dream, fifty years on, will hinge on the degree to which the uneasy relationship between art and education funding resolves itself over the next period.

Our faith in building a new theatre for children has finally paid off. By next autumn, it will be open. But it feels as if, like Rip Van Winkle, we wake up to discover that our – apparently unique – new theatre is in fact now part of a children's theatre landscape which has grown in the interim.

The MacRobert Arts Centre and Imaginate Festival in Scotland – The Ark in Dublin – The Egg in Bath. Even the M6 Company (named after its touring area) now has a new studio in Rochdale. There is the Take Off Festival in the north – the CIAO Festival in the south. In London, Polka Theatre – and now the new Unicorn Theatre. Do these centres and festivals represent something more than just a collection of shiny buildings and showcases? New theatres for children are opening in Stuttgart, Tel Aviv and Vienna. Normandy National Theatre wants to connect with our new theatre. An informal new European network of children's theatres and festivals is emerging.

First let's create a theatre which has its own identity. Great theatres, like the Bouffes du Nord, or Piccolo Teatro, or Moscow Arts Theatre, or Glasgow Citizens all conjure up a particular vision. Let's not make the mistake of all trying to resemble each other. Each theatre company has a distinctive image reflecting its artistic identity. A theatre should follow its own destiny. Let's avoid the curse of the identical high street mall.

Policy

What do writers want to write about? What stories do we want to tell? What do we want to learn about? What do we want to share with our audiences?

Is more better? By producing fewer shows we stand a greater chance of lighting the lights than if we settle for a relentless and rushed stream of work. If we really believe in quality, the cycle of development and growth should take place over a longer period of time. Research and development, longer rehearsals, the opportunity to be playful, time for reflection and revision: all these suggest that we would be better off producing less.

Who needs balance? The idea of creating a balanced programme is potentially deadly. It's a social solution maybe, but not an artistic one. To aim for programmatic balance where each age range gets a show is to get the question the wrong way around. Instead, what excites us? It's invariably true that the best work emerges from our passions and secret desires, not from a socially-engineered timetable. Between a larger auditorium (seating 340) and a studio (seating 120), we can create an interesting dynamic. We've chosen to open the theatre with a new show in the main house, and an installation (made by children) in the studio.

What kind of experiences do we want to create? To ignore balance is to risk falling over. But falling over is an essential part of learning how to stand up. And anyway, while adults can see the pitfalls, children think it's hilarious. Two connected questions have stayed with me.

Practicalities

Can we bring a play for teenagers to your new theatre? Apart from Contact Theatre in Manchester, there are precious few building spaces where work aimed at teenagers is welcome. The idea that work should stop being presented at the age of twelve strikes me as very strange. A seven year old can be a three year old, or a forty-three year old, seven years old. Developmental stages don't necessarily happen in neat, chronological order.

Will they come to a space designated for children? My discussions with the architect from the earliest days revolved around this question. The Ark centre houses an apparent contradiction: the need to respect the right of all children to cultural entitlement, but within the framework of a cultural centre whose architecture does not talk down. I encouraged the architect to juxtapose the rough with the beautiful. Wanting children to be central does not mean excluding everyone else. So we can try to create a place where children, teenagers and adults can coexist and enjoy themselves – even if the accent is on children. I've used the phrase 'a grown-up theatre for children' – the idea that children are growing up themselves. Can we provide a space for them to grow into rather than trap them in an eternal Neverland?

Children consulted. We conducted a consultancy with a group of children from Tower Bridge Primary School – the nearest to the new theatre. A long discussion that took over three years. It was peppered with visits to other theatres, meetings with our architect and his team, work with public artists and various members of our Education Team.

Do we give greater weight to talking with and listening to children? The languages of art and architecture can often reveal more than straight talking. Spatial, descriptive, poetic, metaphorical, dramatic, theatrical, illustrative: all these means might yield a richer conversation. In the preparatory and research stages, in the growth of a project, in the use, shape and life of the building, we need to constantly be provoked by children's ideas. It's not that we should be led by their ideas any more than we should aim to lead them – but we do need to be aware of a child's perspective. Some of the best children's literature and drama has emerged out of playing and storytelling with children.

Peter Pan, *Alice in Wonderland* and Beatrix Potter's tales all grew out of adult artists talking to, writing for and playing with children. There is something here we can learn from and build on. One of our three performing spaces is dedicated to participatory work with and by children. I'd like to think that all spaces in the new theatre will be educational.

Child consultant

Art and Education – Two Sides of the same Theatre

They intermingle and jostle up beside each other. Often, they separate and go their own way. Some years ago, we established a new principle for working on participatory projects – no longer would we work with many children over a short period of time. Rather, we would work with fewer children over a longer period of time. Our drama-led work, rooted in British drama-in-education, will continue to sound the dominant key. The theatre will also offer new possibilities for working with children. The idea of professional artists researching and performing with children will play a significant role in this new venture. Previously, we have not had enough space to bring together our children, their schools and extended families with our artistic projects. But there is another dialogue too. Artists, educationalists, psychologists and cultural producers can learn from each other's work with children. The new theatre offers a focus for a different kind of engagement.

Connections – Dialogue with Practitioners from Abroad

Our first year heralds an important dialogue with great practitioners from Sweden. Three weeks of work across the theatre in the autumn of 2006 will feature Unga Klara, Suzanne Osten, Medea's Children, actors' workshops, dialogue. It's an opportunity to see some great work and also a chance to ask some questions about why and how we do what we do. This mini-season will focus on the ways in which we make work, the assumptions underlying our theatre choices and our approach to children. Swedish companies are responsible for some of our most challenging and artistically exploratory work. Boundaries have been crossed or ignored. Shadows have been cast aside. A refusal to be reduced to 'children's theatre' (with its multiple connotations) can encourage us in Britain to take heart.

In our first year, we are co-producing an English version of *A Doll in her Pocket* for younger children with Teatro delle Briciole from Parma. How can we learn, share the work, hold the moment up for reflection? The world's cultural focus is also tilting eastwards as India and China move to the centre of the world stage. In 2007, we are hosting a Japanese collaboration featuring the work of companies like Kaze-no-ko. An East-West dialogue might explore the purity of forms, a sense of growing alienation from our children, the importance of image and craft. We need to look beyond our own gardens.

Finally – Is there a Renaissance in Theatre for Children in the UK?

Yes – the signs are that a new wave is on the way. In some places it is already happening. A rich mix is envisaged in our new theatre including our own new work, that of other visiting national and UK companies, and work from other cultures. It will take some years before we know where we're heading – and then I hope we'll change direction!

The new Unicorn Theatre opens in London, near Tower Bridge, in Autumn 2005. It will stage a year-round programme of theatre and other events, its own productions and host visiting companies from this country and abroad. It will also run practical research into the questions raised by its repertoire.

Tony Graham was Director of Tag Theatre in Scotland, before taking over as Artistic Director of the Unicorn Theatre.

A CHILD-CENTRED UNICORN

Carl Miller reports on a meeting

A building site near Tower Bridge

Unicorn: What's the point of you?
Child: You should learn not to make personal remarks. It's very rude. I might just as well ask, what's the point of you?
Unicorn: I'm the Unicorn.
Child: I don't think so.
Unicorn: Why ever not?
Child: You don't look like a Unicorn. You look like a building site. Where's your horn?

Unicorn sulks. Pause.

Unicorn: At the moment I look like a building site, but in a few months I'll be a theatre.
Child: Then will you be alive?
Unicorn: Not on my own. I'll need people like you.
Child: People like me?
Unicorn: Children. I need children to live.

Child: Like an ogre?

Unicorn: I don't eat them.

Child: What do you do to them then?

Unicorn: I try and get them to imagine, to feel, to think...

Child: Doesn't sound very likely to me. You're not a child are you?

Unicorn: Do I look like a child?

Child: About as much as you look like a Unicorn.

Unicorn: I was designed with a group of child consultants. From that school over there.

Child: Well... that's something I suppose. So what do you do?

Unicorn: That's a good question.

Child: That's what people always say when they don't want to tell you something.

Unicorn: I know when I'll be built. But that's not a finish. That's a start.

Child: Is that a riddle?

Unicorn: No. It's just that I'm not really a building. I'm a space.

Child: More riddles. Why do children in books always meet characters who love riddles?

Unicorn: Can we imagine worlds which are different?

Child: Why are these only questions for children?

Unicorn: They're not.

Child: So do you want adults to come here as well?

Unicorn: Yes. Children and adults share the world after all.

Child: But we usually come second.

Unicorn: Yes. That's how I've got to be different.

Child: How will you do that?

Unicorn: It says here I'll make and present 'theatre with the child's perspective at its centre'.

Child: What does that mean?

Unicorn: 'The images we create, the stories we tell, the ideas or emotions we explore and the forms in which we work must engage with children above all.' That's what they say.

Child: Wait a minute. How can you know what a child's perspective is? Are all of the people making theatre here children?

Unicorn: Some of them will be. But you're right, mostly they won't. But all those who aren't children once were, weren't they?

Child: Nice try. But that doesn't make you a children's theatre.
Unicorn: Did I say I was one?
Child: Didn't you? I thought I'd heard you were.
Unicorn: A children's theatre. Maybe that's an impossibility.
Child: So is a unicorn.

Pause.

Child: Are you going to disappear then?
Unicorn: No.

Carl Miller is Unicorn Literary Manager

'It's not like watching TV. Everyone in that big space is alive, and everyone is focused on one central activity ... the audience contributes their attention, their silence, their laughter, their applause, their respect. And they contribute their imagination too.'

Philip Pullman, Unicorn Theatre Newsletter

POLKA – A DEDICATED CHILDREN'S THEATRE

A place for children to laugh, to be moved, to play and share the magic of theatre. Annie Wood and Stephen Midlane highlight recent projects.

Polka started as a touring company. Richard Gill had a policy of bringing craft and colour to productions and wanted to do the same to a theatre building as a home to the productions. A disused church hall in Wimbledon, in South London, was found and converted. In 1979, Polka Theatre opened with a main auditorium, studio theatre, café, playground, toyshop and exhibition space. It became a popular attraction for the high value productions and the exceptional environment in which they were staged. Once established in its own space, the Company quickly began to diversify and extend the number of writers, directors and puppeteers with whom the company worked.

In 1988, Vicky Ireland joined Polka as the second Artistic Director. Productions, now predominantly actor-based and driven by quality scriptwriting, widened in both content and form. Polka worked with some of Britain's leading writers, including Alan Ayckbourn, Philip Pullman, David Holman, Jamila Gavin, Malorie Blackman, Charles Way and Mike Kenny. Vicky Ireland's devotion to quality playwriting was also reflected in 2001 in Polka's New Writing Programme. Importantly, Polka also provides a London venue for touring children's theatre companies from the UK and abroad.

In 2002, Annie Wood was appointed as the third Artistic Director, having worked extensively in children's theatre in the UK and abroad. Her productions of *The Red Balloon* and *Martha* had both received international acclaim, each touring North America. A new development since Annie Wood's arrival has been to extend the age range of the audience. Polka has now staged three plays for teenagers, and in 2005 will produce its very own production for babies. Annie says of the theatre:

> 'My vision for Polka is as much about the space as it is about the programme. It is rare to have a building exclusively for children. We must explore the creative potential of the space. Polka is a place where, as you walk through the door, you feel welcome. Toddlers know it's all right to crawl around and explore. Parents

know it's a safe environment, with baby-changing, a buggy park, and friendly staff. Older children get involved through our participatory work, but also in our book corner, in the garden and the playground. I've even seen teenagers at first cautious of the space, then queuing to go down the slide!

The only predictable element is the quality of the work we produce. Our programme is for all ages and offers a variety of drama, dance pieces, the best new writing for children, adaptations of contemporary and classic stories. We host a writing festival each year – and even stand-up comedy for kids. Polka is a place to play, to laugh, to be moved, and share the magic of theatre with family and friends.'

Theatre on the Main Stage: Young Europe

Co-produced by Polka Theatre and Company of Angels, we have introduced plays for young audiences by European playwrights not seen in the UK before.

Kadouma's Island by Joel Jouanneau and Marie–Claire Le Pvec (translated by Alan Pollock). For children aged 6+. A fantastical exploration of the legacy of colonialism played out between a black man and a white woman. Set on a tiny island, this gentle comedy touched on grief and the healing power of love.

Little Angels by Marco Balliano (translated by Theresa Ariosto). For children aged 8+. The story of a man and a woman who meet under the glow of an isolated street lamp. *Little Angels* uses lots of physical hi-

PHOTO: ROBERT WORKMAN

The meeting

jinks, comedy and snappy dialogue to show how when you're faced with nothing but trouble, the power of love and friendship gets you through.

Sweetpeter by John Retallack and Usifu Jalloh for young people 12+. A hard-hitting and surreal examination of slavery. *Sweetpeter* is born into slavery, and over several reincarnations lives out the struggle for liberation in Africa and the horrors of civil war. The play was highly physical, played out by a wonderful ensemble of black and white actors, and had a real impact on the teenage audience.

A company of six actors played the three plays for six months at Polka and on tour. This project was the first very ambitious step in our programme of presenting European work – we are planning to co-produce other texts with Company of Angels.

Children meet a Family at home in a transformed Foyer Space

Best Behaviour. For children 5+. A devised show by guest director Mark Storer. The production used a highly visual, non-narrative approach to performance. The theme – things that are said in family

Bath-time on stage

life – 'You're driving your mother up the wall', 'Sister's getting too big for her boots', 'Dad's like a bear with a sore head'. The Polka foyer was transformed – the floor covered with black and white linoleum, a staircase going up to the ceiling, a bath, chairs and tables suspended from the wall. The audience of eighty were seated on the floor, right in the middle of the action, with glass cases surrounding them. The actors literally hung from ceilings, climbed up the walls, stepped in and out of glass cases and moved around close to the audience.

There was no obvious narrative, and at times more than one scene would happen at the same time. We see photos of the family going to bed, mother hanging from the ceiling as she bathes her youngest son. We witness the characters discovering what it was like to kiss, their goldfish dying, when mother lied, learning how to shave, listening in on adult conversations from the top of the stairs.

Children meet a Giant in a Garden in the Studio Theatre

The Selfish Giant – Oscar Wilde's fairy tale for the under 5's. The action started in the foyer where the children meet Spring. The aim was actively to involve the audience.

Spring asks the children to help her plant seeds in the Giant's garden, so the children enter into the garden in character clutching the seeds. The Studio was completely transformed into a garden and the children sat on the floor. They participated in the show, playing the part of the children who enter the garden while the Giant is away. When the Giant returns he throws them all out, resulting in Spring, Summer and Autumn not visiting the garden anymore and Winter moving in for good. As the garden freezes over a little boy's balloon flies over the wall of the garden, and into the hands of the Giant. He lets the children come back in to the garden and they make it lovely once more. Then he leaves to find the little boy and to give the balloon back to him. The Giant leaves the child-audience to look after his garden, and a case filled with magic giant seeds. When they plant them, flowers fall from the sky – magic!

The boy's balloon

Education Programme

Education is central to all of Polka Theatre's productions. We are dedicated to improving access to theatre, and our projects are for *all* children. We welcome Special Needs school groups to Polka with a scheme that we have created called Arts Access. We provide multi-sensory work packs, to stimulate further related work. We offer workshops after school and during the holidays for three to seventeen year olds (including hearing-impaired children).

Playgrounding

Richard Shannon, Director of New Writing, has set up *Playgrounding* as a script development programme. Selected writers who would not have considered writing for young audiences attend free master classes. They then submit an idea for a play in the form of a one page synopsis and five pages of dialogue. Each script is then workshopped in a school with the appropriate age range. Over the course of the project, the writers work with established children's dramatists and theatre artists, including designers and composers. The programme culminates in a festival of workshop productions, open to the public.

Polka's Mission

- to inspire children's imagination and creativity through the production and presentation of excellent and innovative theatre
- to provide a welcoming and attractive theatre environment for such work
- to celebrate all children, and relish cultural diversity

Annie Wood is the Artistic Director and Stephen Midlane, is the Administrator at Polka Theatre.

REGIONAL THEATRE – Building New Audiences of Young People

Steve Ball describes the Education and Outreach Programme at Birmingham Repertory Theatre – opening doors to the community, involving schools in creating a mainstage production for children.

Theatre in Birmingham

Not many people can claim to have a job which combines all of their passions. So I'm lucky that I can pursue three of mine – theatre, education and Birmingham!

England's second city is recognised as a model for using the Arts and Culture as part of its Regeneration Programme. We boast the internationally recognised Birmingham Royal Ballet and Symphony Orchestra – and a range of community arts organisations which reflect the cultural diversity of our thriving city. Birmingham was the first provincial city in the last century to set up a Repertory Theatre housing a local professional theatre company. 'The Rep' occupies a prominent site in the civic square, with one of the largest stages outside London. It also has a studio theatre, The Door, dedicated to the development and production of new writing.

I had led two educational theatre companies based in the city. One of my frustrations then was not being recognised by the city's principal producing theatre – Birmingham Rep. There was a suspicion that the Artistic Director believed engaging with communities, or schools, would serve as a distraction from the main purpose of the organisation – to produce plays. This misses the opportunity to promote high quality theatre productions as education resources. I jumped at the chance to join the Rep, not just to utilise my local experience, but to prove the educational potential that a Regional Producing Theatre provides.

Regional Theatres

Despite some excellent examples of good practice, education in regional theatres has often been ghettoised and marginalised. Many do not enjoy the close, hard won relationships with schools and communities that small-scale and Theatre-in-Education companies have established. In some regional theatres, Education is part of the Marketing Department, principally concerned with getting 'bums on seats'. In others, there is an Education Team, but it operates at arm's length from the rest of the theatre, in a separate building, producing work with no connection to the theatre's mainstage programme. There often exists a tension between the 'arts development' and 'audience development' roles of Education departments, with relatively few addressing both aims.

Key Education Commitments

My first task was to identify Education as central to management.

Quality: production and artistic values for education activities are as high as for mainstage productions.

Social Inclusion: positive action to involve all sections of the community, recognising invisible barriers surrounding the organisation.

Lifelong Learning: providing education opportunities for very young children, school pupils, students and elders.

Celebration and Promotion of Cultural Diversity: in the city and region; in all activities, including main stage productions.

Working in Partnership: with other organisations to give additional value.

On the basis of this, Education Team members run:

- Workshops in schools and Theatre Days: Students come to the theatre, meet the production team, observe rehearsals, and tour backstage before a performance.
- Teacher Courses/Skills Exchange Days: Teachers participate in drama workshops, and advise us on resource packs.
- Young Rep: Our youth theatre rehearses four satellite groups in neighbourhoods across the city, who perform on stage at the Rep each year.
- First Stages: Theatre for three to seven year olds. We produce and co-produce work for children with local companies such as Sister Tree, and international companies such as Teatro Kismet from Bari in Italy.

The Local Community: One of the most challenging statistics that I encountered was that very few of the residents had ever set foot in the building, or regarded it as part of their community. Inspired by West Yorkshire Playhouse's Hey Days programme, we consulted these local residents about what arts activities they would like to happen at the theatre. Drawing and Painting classes came top of the list! A tutor now runs weekly workshops in our Front of House spaces. This term their work will focus upon our mainstage production of *The Crucible*, with local residents sitting in rehearsals doing life drawings of the actors. Their work will culminate in an exhibition in the foyer.

Rep's Children: At the other end of the age spectrum, every baby born in the City Hospital in 2004 will get a free theatre experience every year for ten years, involving families from inner city neighbourhoods. We will produce a multi-sensory theatre programme for babies and their young siblings.

Schools Develop a Show for the Main Stage

A project fulfilling both arts development and audience development objectives was *The Shooky*. Funded and developed with Creative Partnerships, this project began as a scheme for ten teachers from Birmingham primary schools who spent a day shadowing our senior management team. The teachers then formed a production company, were given a sizable budget, and a remit to recruit a writer and a director for a new production for primary school children. Peter Wynne-Willson and Toby Frow were appointed as writer and director, and spent one month working closely with 250 children from five primary and special schools in the city. They collected ideas and themes that Peter synthesised into *The Shooky*, a magical tale performed by six professional actors about characters who lived in an open space in the city. Meanwhile the teachers devised the marketing strategy and resource pack for the production.

This turns the commissioning process on its head! Rather than one Artistic Director deciding what should happen on our main stage, the decisions were given to young children from across Birmingham. The children's investment in the production was huge, and the rewards for them and us were enormous. It is a genuine 'Creative Partnership', one in which we as theatre practitioners had as much to learn from children, teachers and schools, as they had to learn from us.

PHOTO: ALAN WOOD

The Shooky Company

The Future

It's still relatively early days, but we are as an organisation beginning to prove that the dual roles of producing high quality theatre, and developing active learning opportunities are not mutually exclusive – but mutually beneficial.

Steve Ball was Director of Language Alive TIE and Catalyst Theatre in Health Education before becoming Education Officer for Birmingham Repertory Theatre.

COME IN OUT OF THE RAIN!

More than just a building – a day in the life of the Sherman Theatre Cardiff

Philip Clark and Margaret Jones report on a theatre dedicated to performances for children and young people – an active Youth Theatre – and links to schools, the community and internationally.

It's a damp, grey, 'missly' Saturday morning in rainy Cardiff and we're trudging up a wide tree-lined street, the pavement slippery with fallen leaves, but we don't mind! We have the taste of excited anticipation in our mouths as we approach the theatre. On opening the doors a swell of sounds envelops us like a warm blanket; bright colours, a spacious foyer, full of children and adults; little children and grown up children! 'Saturday Young Scene' is our regular season of performances by Travelling Light, or Theatre Alibi, Theatre Centre, and Unicorn Theatre – individuals and companies, from clowns to puppeteers.

Children and parents with performers in foyer

The Sherman's Young People's Policy

It begins with the very young and sort of ends at – as long as you enjoy the work we programme we don't mind your age! The programme of visiting company performance extends to plays for and by young adults – Red Ladder, Asian Theatre School, Forkbeard Fantasy, Graeae Theatre Company, contemporary dance, stand-up comedy, Wales-based companies performing in English and in Welsh, from classics to new writing – all check and balance with our mission to place the act of theatre-going firmly on the leisure agenda of the young, along side cinema, pop concerts and sporting facilities.

In 2005, Cardiff celebrates its centenary as a city, and the Sherman Theatre Company will produce some of the top children's playwrights: Mike Kenny's *Swan Songs* – a new play about the life and stories of Hans Christian Andersen; Charles Way's *Merlin and the Cave of Dreams*. Alongside these children's productions we will also present two new plays for teenagers by Gary Owen and D.J. Britton on the main stage, and on tour in Wales.

Education, Youth and Participation Department

In the dance studio/rehearsal room next door there is a further hive of activity. We run twelve youth theatre groups, with over one hundred and eighty members, aged between ten and twenty-five years. These young people participate in weekly workshops (including three Welsh Language workshops). The Youth Theatre perform in full-scale productions, street theatre, end-of-term shows and international exchanges – the most recent of these being with the Czech Republic.

Summer Schools: *Alice – a State of Mind* 2003, *Frankenstein* 2004. Using music, movement and film these push the boundaries of expectations for theatre by young people. We also host the National Youth Theatre of Wales annual production.

Acting Out Cardiff!

This is an educational and performance initiative aimed at top secondary school pupils, taking them out of the classroom to give them hands-on experience and accreditation in a professional arts environment. This project enables young people to gain confidence in themselves, to gain skills for life, and to express individuality whilst working as a team. A local head teacher said: 'If only every school in

Wales had a Sherman Theatre attached to it!' The young people work towards small productions – in the rehearsal room to Sherman staff and as the young people move on in the course, in our studio theatre. They work with the Sherman tutors and outside tutors ranging from circus skills, to video artists.

The culminating project is one which they take out to schools. This year's project is *No Man's Land*. Three months devising the play, scriptwriting, designing and rehearsing, pay off and the group feel an enormous sense of achievement and enjoy taking on the responsibility of being peer educators. An education pack is written with the students for schools. Extracts are performed to delegates at the Careers Teachers' Annual Conference. Students speak to the efficacy of vocational learning through the arts. They receive grades from Edexcel for the BTEC Certificate in Performing Arts. This project was presented with a Youth Work in Wales Excellence Award in November 2004.

Community Outreach

We are also establishing a programme which gives access to the arts for a wider range of the Cardiff community, by initiating participatory projects and events, both at the Sherman and in the communities themselves. The department is focused on inclusion for young people, and members of the community who may feel that the cultural arts activity of the city is not for them. As well as working locally, we are also establishing international links bringing together young people, artists and teachers from all over the world to be part of Cardiff's cultural activity. Venue 3, a small performance space in the upstairs gallery, suitable for rehearsed readings and script-in-hand performances is offered to writers, directors and actors who want to experiment with new work in front of an audience. With a staff of only thirty supporting this extensive programme of work, we also work on Royal Welsh College of Music and Drama arts management, acting, stage manage-ment and design, and music courses. We provide Youth Theatre Studies for Arts in the Community at The University of Glamorgan.

The Future

We have survived years of reducing grant aid and missed European funding because the borderline is ten yards from the Sherman – and we're on the *wrong* side! Now we have plans to extend the building on the Welsh Arts Council pilot programme, and feel at last that there is hope for us to create the Young People's Theatre we have always dreamt of. Here's hoping!

Meanwhile downstairs, in the basement rehearsal room, our award-winning professional Sherman Theatre Company, is in rehearsal for the world premiere of Cardiff born, Roald Dahl's – *Danny, the Champion of the World.*

Oh, and by the way, it's not always grey and 'missly' in Cardiff!

Philip Clark is Director of the Sherman Theatre and Margaret Jones is General Manager.

4. WRITING FOR CHILDREN AND YOUNG AUDIENCES

TWENTY FIVE YEARS ON WHIRLIGIG – before and since

What led David Wood into writing and directing plays for children's audiences in large theatres, his commitment to its importance, and how he developed the craft skills.

Before Whirligig

When I wrote my first play for children in 1967 I had no idea children's theatre would take over my life. Little did I think that nearly four decades later I would have written more than sixty plays and adaptations for young audiences, produced and directed many of them for my own touring children's theatre company, and helped to pioneer the presentation of plays for children in both middle-scale civic theatres, and large commercial touring venues.

Rewards and Risks in Children's Theatre

My main passion is producing large-scale plays, using all the theatrical tricks at my disposal to entertain children, make them laugh, make them think, trigger their imaginations and convince them that the theatre is an exciting place where magical stories unfold and interesting ideas are explored. This is, was, and ever shall be, I believe, a mightily worthwhile challenge. And it never gets easier. Experience helps, but the more I do, the more challenging each project proves to be! But, as all children's practitioners know, when we get it right, it's the most rewarding feeling. The whole-hearted response of an audience of children is so much more tangible and exciting than the measured sophistication of an audience of adults. The openness, honesty and volatility of children make every performance a roller-coaster ride. The actors are working on a knife edge.

And if we get it wrong, if the play isn't working, children let us know soon enough! No sitting quietly, though bored, and clapping politely at the end, as adults do. Children, when uninvolved, will talk, shuffle and ask to go to the lavatory. I sometimes feel that my entire life's work has been dedicated to attempting to rivet them to their seats, unable to take their eyes off the stage for fear of missing something. Finding ways to lessen the loo-count has undoubtedly contributed to the development of my writing technique, and the way I direct the plays and the actors.

Over the years, I have been aware that my approach, particularly in the larger theatres, is seen as 'commercial' by some fellow practitioners. I have often felt somewhat apart from the national and international children's theatre movement. My plays have rarely been seen at children's theatre festivals, as they are too large to travel economically – cast too big – too much time to get-in and get-out – need facilities for lighting and sound (sometimes flying scenery). They cannot visit schools or art centres. In spite of these drawbacks, many of my plays, if not my productions, have been seen all over the world so I have been getting something right. Because I work on a large scale, perhaps my UK colleagues have felt that I don't value the work of small-scale companies. Not true. Some of the best children's plays I have seen involve just two or three actors working in a small space, with the minimum of scenery and props. Such work is inspirational, educational and wonderfully imaginative – but it is simply not my style.

First Productions

Once I went to a big commercial pantomime and found myself despairing at how thin the storyline was. The comedian walked downstage, leant over the footlights and joked, 'Let's get the children out of here, then we can get started'. I left thinking of how little real theatre for children was on offer. Occasional productions of *Alice in Wonderland*, *The Wind in the Willows*, *The Wizard of Oz* were available, but little original writing, and virtually nothing to be seen at any time except Christmas.

I was acting and directing at the Swan Theatre, Worcester, a medium-sized repertory theatre in middle England. Asked to produce Saturday morning children's theatre, I encouraged the actors in the company to join me in presenting storytelling, magic and music. Then I wrote the Christmas play. This was the start! The following year I wrote – *The Owl and the Pussycat went to See* based on the verses and stories of Edward Lear and the reaction of the children to this was wildly enthusiastic. Watching from the back of the auditorium, performance after performance, witnessing the excitement and the total involvement, convinced me that I had found my niche! I managed to get the play on in London the following year, directed it this time, and thus embarked on what became my life's work.

More plays and productions followed through the late 60's and early 70's. There was even a commercial tour of *The Owl and the Pussycat* by a young Cameron Mackintosh. For the first time the play was seen in the large touring houses, and, to my pleasant surprise, even in fifteen hundred seaters, it still worked. Twelve in the cast. Colourful sets. One musician. Lots of lighting effects. My aim was to make children's theatre part of the mainstream fabric of the British theatre scene, not a ghetto activity, barred from proper theatres and restricted to small venues, and the Christmas slot.

'Commercial' versus 'Educational' Children's Theatre

The TIE movement had begun, with spectacular success, at the Belgrade Theatre, Coventry; actor/teachers were going into schools presenting project plays on contemporary themes. Theatre was becoming an educational tool. Other TIE companies sprung up; evangelists from Coventry spread the word and the work to other towns. As an actor with Watford TIE company, I had enjoyed presenting a play in schools about the Tay Bridge disaster, then discussing with the audience the notion of collective responsibility but I wanted these same children to go to the theatre in a theatre building. I encouraged schools we had visited to come and see us on the stage. Some purists felt that theatres were middle-class institutions. The word 'magic' had to them become a dirty word, not what theatre for children should be about. I have to say this saddened me. Children should enjoy seeing story acted out in a theatre!

Qualities for Success

In 1976, I wrote *The Gingerbread Man*, which became my most popular play. Ten West End seasons, many repertory seasons, UK tours, been shown on television, and published in book form. Performed widely in Germany and Japan, it opened in China in 2004. Cynically, I can explain its success by saying it has only six in the cast, and is performed on one basic set. But I think it also has other qualities.

We all live on a Welsh Dresser in a kitchen. I'm the Cuckoo in the Clock and I'm losing my voice. I'm a newly-baked Gingerbread Man (an innocent, and at first anarchic, child, really). I help him find it! Salt-pot, Pepper-mill, lonely Tea-bag and scavenging Mouse both help and hinder.

The play uses scale – giant props that children love. The characters are mainly inanimate objects, some with animal connections. They live in their own world – a microcosm of ours. Themes of death (Cuckoo might get thrown away by the human Big Ones, who are heard but never seen) and isolation, as well as the celebration of community life, seem to keep audiences worldwide interested and entertained. It is not very deep, but I believe it triggers imaginations and gives pleasure. The reason there were six actors was financial. In the eight years since I had written *The Owl and the Pussycat*, the average cast number, even for a regional Christmas show, had been forced down to half the number possible in 1968. Ever since, I have rarely been asked to write for more than a cast of eight or ten.

On the Whirligig

By 1979 I had a dream! Rather than produce one-off productions for four-week seasons in London and elsewhere, or for Repertory Theatre Christmas shows, I wanted to tour, to play full weeks at theatres all over the UK, mainly for school parties. After a successful pilot tour, my dream came true – my partners and I founded Whirligig Theatre, which became 'the national children's touring theatre' – and ran for twenty-five years.

Sponsorship came initially from *Clarks* Shoes. Our London show-case for many years was the prestigious Sadler's Wells, where we even managed to get national newspaper reviews. We played most of the major UK theatres. The Whirligig name became trusted and we didn't have to rely on established titles or adaptations of well-known books. The announcement that 'Whirligig is coming!' was sufficient to ensure full houses. Funding, however, was a problem. *Clarks* Shoes left us after four years. The Arts Council Touring Department became our main source of income, but frustratingly they only gave one-off project funding, not guaranteed regular revenue funding. So planning ahead was impossible, as was expansion. We wanted to commission new plays and foster new writers, but we never had the money to do it. Whirligig only produced plays by David Wood – I could, and regularly did, waive my royalties if we had financial problems.

In the early years, the plays were an extension of my story adventures work.

The Plotters of Cabbage Patch Corner: Set in a garden (large props again), featured a cast of insects.

Nutcracker Sweet: All about nuts! – Monkeynut, Gypsy Brazil, Kernel Walnut and Old Ma Coconut, working in a Nutty May Fair, and threatened by the ghastly Chocolate Squirter, who wanted to transform them into a luxury chocolate assortment.

The Ideal Gnome Expedition: The adventures of two garden gnomes, who experience the dangers and delights of the concrete jungle of the big city.

The plays were mainly 'entertaining', but did tackle issues, and by now we had taken a leaf from the TIE book, and offered an Education Pack and Teachers' Seminars.

Cross-over between Children's Theatre and Education. In the 80's I felt I developed as a playwright. The divisions between children's theatre and educational theatre eased. TIE and children's theatre were assimilating some of each other's methods, and this was generally mutually beneficial. A cross-fertilisation was taking place. For my own part, I wrote two plays with Conservation as their theme:

The Selfish Shellfish: Rock pool creatures battle against an invading oil slick.

The See-Saw Tree: The inhabitants of an ancient oak tree are in danger of losing their home when a supermarket is scheduled to be built, necessitating the chopping down of the tree. I believe that children got the point through identifying with the animal characters – children often prefer animals to human beings – and became involved (using audience participation) in saving the day. Maybe the solutions offered in the plays are too 'easy', and don't really reflect the harshness of real life, but certainly the response in the children's letters and pictures, and the teachers' comments, suggested they worked on both levels – the theatre experience, and the issue awareness.

Save The Human went even further; this was a play about animal rights. Rather than depicting grizzly scenes of beagles smoking cigarettes in laboratories, I used role reversal to make the point. In the future, when human beings have ruined everything with wars and pollution, animals 'rule the world' and employ the few remaining human beings as work-humans or pets. Becky Bear tries to 'Save the Human' in a huge campaign.

The plays were imaginatively staged, with a more physical style of acting. Music played a major part, both songs and incidental music. And our actors were not beginners using children's theatre as a stepping-stone to 'real' (adult) theatre. They were experienced, dedicated practitioners, who relished working for young audiences, many regular members of our team. So, by the late 80's I really felt we were progressing.

Financing Theatre for Children

Whirligig was never set up as a charity, but we were certainly not a commercial company! We budgeted to break even, and sometimes that was hard. Like other companies, we were almost killed off by the Education Reform Act of 1988. Our advanced school bookings at Sadler's Wells dropped from 7,000 to 4,000. Many civic theatres, who had formerly included children's theatre at a low seat price in their regular programming, as a service to their communities, found that they could no longer afford to rob Peter to pay Paul. Balancing the losses on a sell-out children's show does not match the big profit from a touring adult musical. Each show had to pay its way. Whirligig became side-lined because theatres took in more commercial profitable product.

West End Productions

I decided to explore other avenues. A commercial company (but one of integrity) asked me to adapt and direct Roald Dahl's very popular book, *The BFG (Big Friendly Giant)*. I went ahead, using my regular Whirligig team (design, choreography, music). It became a major success story, with tours to huge audiences, and three West End seasons. And – very significantly – the introduction of early evening performances. School groups came in the morning or afternoon. The family audience came for the evening performance. Ten performances

PHOTO-DEE CONWAY

Mice in *The Witches*

a week. Theatre managements were happy now because their bars and restaurants did good business! We also did not have to share the theatre with an adult attraction. Some of my worse near-nervous breakdown moments had been trying desperately not to compromise the quality of our daytime shows. The producer always assumed the evening production was far more important than ours.

The BFG was not a cop-out! It is a valid theatre experience, not a commercial exploitation. It led to a string of similar plays and productions – six Roald Dahl adaptations in all. *The Witches* is the best known. Meanwhile the pressures on Whirligig increased. We needed big titles, but didn't feel they fitted our credo. An exception was *Babe, The Sheep-Pig*, based on Dick King-Smith's book *The Sheep-Pig*, source of the successful movie *Babe*. We financed this with sponsorship from Barclays Bank; it was a co-production with the Library Theatre, Manchester and the Birmingham Hippodrome. It was very well received, fifteen local children in the cast playing a flock of sheep.

The Whirligig comes to a halt

After twenty-five years, we decided to rest Whirligig, having achieved much if not all of what we had aimed for. Nowadays there is much more product around for the theatres. Many more practitioners actually want to work in theatre for children. And there is more money available from the funding bodies to support the work. I am now writing for other companies including Oxford Playhouse, Sherman Theatre, Birmingham Stage Company and Unicorn Theatre.

Writing and Directing for Children

One basic premise to remember is that I am writing for children, not for myself. That doesn't mean playing down. It means taking note of what children like, are interested in and respond to.

Story, magic, colour, music, animals – and action. Children love stories. A story well told will hold their attention and trigger their imaginations. Children prefer to watch things happen rather than people talking about them.

The theme of justice is important to children; by this I don't necessarily mean morality, right and wrong, rather the fact that children become emotionally involved when a character is being treated unfairly. The story of *Cinderella* is a classic and universally popular example.

Two important virtues: **Pace** – doesn't necessarily mean speed. It means keeping the story going in an immediate and exciting way. Just as good children's authors don't, like some adult authors, spend four pages telling us the sun has come out, a children's playwright needs to deftly move the story forward. **Clarity** – does not mean we should be simplistic; it is just a recognition of the fact that to stop the children becoming bored, they must be able to clearly understand what is going on. Cul-de-sac sub-plots confuse. The main through storyline is paramount.

Just as in classic books for children, a touch of melodrama, and the use of heightened characters often helps, the stories shouldn't be mundane. The characters should be broadly drawn, though not caricatures. Often I have come up with a basic idea – for example creatures living in a rock pool – and then set about thinking of what could be the worst thing that might happen to them. How might they react? Roald Dahl did this. His witches don't just cast the odd spell to make someone vanish, they want to eradicate all the children in the whole world! A huge idea, made more potent by the fact that the witches' target is children, the very audience at which the book is aimed.

When looking for a book to adapt I am looking for some of my suggested ingredients plus what I can only describe as 'theatricality'. Fantasy from reality often provides this. *Peter Pan* is the classic example. A normal (admittedly Edwardian middle-class normal) family's bedtime is transformed by the arrival of a magical flying boy, who transports the children through the window to Neverland. From a normal picnic, Alice goes down the rabbit hole and emerges into a strange, illogical world. The Narnia children go through the wardrobe towards danger and adventure.

Use of scale adds to theatricality. Little Sophie is taken by the BFG to a world of child-eating giants. My own Gingerbread Man kitchen characters are threatened by the human Big Ones. Products of a vivid imagination with themes of life and death, yet often injected with humour.

Theatrical Language

Translating a story from page to stage, whether it be my own story or that of another writer, involves finding a 'theatrical language' to faithfully deliver it to the audience, asking:

- can I use doubling or trebling? (sometimes play construction becomes almost mathematical, to allow for actors to make quick changes)
- can songs be used to further the action rather than delay it?
- can the scene changes be fluent?
- can I find a cliff-hanger for the interval, to leave the audience excited to know what happens next?
- must I change the structure of the book to make it work theatrically?
- can I introduce new characters at strategic points to maintain interest?
- do I need an exciting climax towards the end before the story resolves?
- are there sufficient opportunities for interesting lighting and sound?
- can audience participation make a valuable contribution?
- do the characters offer variety in the way they speak, look, move?

– would puppets be appropriate?

– will mime and choreography feature?

Directing my plays has taught me how to direct actors

Sincerity: If an actor feels demeaned by playing, say, a slug or a saltpot, he had best not be employed. The actors need to have retained a sense of wonder, almost innocence. Any sign of cynicism will be instantly spotted by the audience. Children won't sit there thinking the actors are being insincere, they will simply turn off.

Scale: I direct the actors in a stylised manner to reflect the heightened nature of the characters. 'Big' performances, brave performances are often necessary.

Focus: I often freeze those actors not playing a major part in a scene. A child's range of vision is not as wide as an adult's. Children often move their heads from side to side when watching the stage. My job is to always make sure they are looking where I want them to look.

Truth: Actors sometimes approach the job thinking that a pervasive atmosphere of enforced jollity is required. But 'bigness' does not mean 'silly'. Sincerity and truth, acting 'in the now', taking it seriously, not coming out of character, and, as it were, winking at the audience, is vital. Complicity with the audience is one thing, patronising them is another.

Reponses: Actors must realise that acting to children is more of a roller-coaster ride than performing to adults. Voices from the auditorium may be heard – 'I don't like that one!', or, 'She's funny!' Crying infants may well interrupt, forced to stay on the laps of the doting parents, who are determined that their offspring will eventually enjoy the experience for which they are probably far too young.

Techniques I have discovered to hold an audience

Suddenlies. The equivalent of the page-turning moments in good books. They are the staccato interruptions on bedside screens in hospitals. They are moments when a wandering audience can be jolted back. A sudden new idea, a surprise, a new character entering, a sound cue, a lighting cue, a musical sting, a variety of tone, a change of mood. My aim is to have several 'suddenlies' on every page of text.

They – not too obviously I hope – are intended to keep the play alive and the audience alert. I am trying to prevent them from getting distracted by making it impossible for them to take their eyes off the stage for fear of missing something.

Making Positive Statements. Something I suggest to actors who have to say something negative, for example, 'I've never been so unhappy in my life'. The naturalistic way is to play it inwardly and negatively. But if spoken positively, with energy, it becomes an outward pronouncement that helps to retain the character's link with the audience. It helps keep the scene aloft and alive. It prevents the scene 'dropping'.

These aids have hopefully stopped many children in my audiences turning off – and going to the lavatory. A crude system of evaluation, but to me an invaluable one.

In Conclusion – Children Need Theatre

My faith in children's theatre in the middle-scale and large theatres is undiminished. I still believe children's theatre must be done 'properly', using all the theatrical techniques and tricks at our disposal. I still believe in the magic of fantasy stories. But I also try harder to come to terms with some of the big issues and 'difficult' subjects – but always in a theatrical and entertaining way. It saddens me when people still think of children's theatre as being candyfloss, and lacking in substance or content. It simply isn't true.

The future of live theatre depends on a healthy children's theatre, introducing children to a theatre-going habit, enjoyed into adulthood. The purveyors of adult theatre should cherish and nurture the work we do, to promulgate the idea of theatre as a leisure activity. I wish that the splendid new writing we are witnessing for smaller-scale children's theatre could extend to more opportunities for writers who want to provide work for the larger spaces. Why isn't the National Theatre more proactive in this? Or The Royal Shakespeare Company? Children are entitled to it. It still works, in spite of competition from computer games and videos. The communal experience is much more memorable and life-affirming, than the solo experience in front of a small screen. Children still need stories, traditional and modern. They still respond to the immediacy and excitement of live theatre.

We need more training for actors, writers and directors in the craft of children's theatre. Most of my generation of practitioners learnt by doing it. We were never trained. Some of us should be passing on

PHOTO: DEE CONWAY

The Sheep-Pig

what we have learnt. Children's theatre should be perceived as a real opportunity, an accepted branch of theatre in which to work, not just a poor, second-division area of theatre in which to cut one's teeth or mark time. It isn't easy! It is arguably the most difficult theatre of all. We need theatre managers to put children's theatre high on the list, newspaper critics to attend productions as regularly as adult shows. Funding bodies to recognise it costs as much to put on as adult theatre, but yields less revenue, because of the necessary low seat price.

For me, children's theatre has been a career, a challenge, a frustration, a passion. The rewards (not always financial) have been huge – there is nothing, no nothing, like sitting in a full house of children, listening, laughing, thinking and truly enjoying themselves.

David Wood has been termed by the theatre critic of The Times newspaper – 'the national children's dramatist'.

SOCIALLY-AWARE PLAYS FOR YOUNG AUDIENCES

David Holman retraces his journey in developing the skills and awareness to tackle challenging themes and topics for young people's theatre.

In 1970 I was invited by the newly-formed and innovative Theatre-in-Education Company at the Coventry Belgrade Theatre, to write for them. I could hardly have imagined that, thirty years later, I would still be writing for young audiences with my work performed in dozens of countries. My interest was the new film movements – Italian neo-realism, Ken Loach's British film. But I was looking for a new direction and Theatre-in-Education was a recently-developed initiative.

Participatory Theatre and Social History

I was fascinated by the TIE team's dramatic exploration of the issues facing a fictional newly de-colonised country – *The Emergent African Game*. It used participation to involve the young audience in the political and social decisions the peoples of Kenya, Tanganyika, and many countries were having to make in those years. I was amazed that such material was being developed for young audiences. Theatre visits into schools which clearly had nothing to do with the conventional curriculum were something I would have loved to have experienced myself.

I saw another programme devised by the Bolton Octagon Theatre Company – *Poverty Knocks*. It also used participation to enable the pupils to explore the effects on ordinary people's lives of the radical political movement known as Chartism. The children and teachers had been provided with material about the day-to-day life of their forbears in early nineteenth century Bolton. Children of their age (eleven and twelve) would not have been attending school. They would have been working. The length of the working day was a crucial matter for them. It was such visceral issues that the programme explored. When the costumed actors arrived, the by-then quite knowledgeable children were thrown into this world of work, and the political turbulence of the time. As the action and the story swept along there were decisions to be made. The children, with an Actor-Teacher 'contact character,' made them. To resist an overbearing foreman – or not? To speak up for a mistreated workmate – or not?

Documentary Themes and Active Research

While the acting company were in schools, I was actively looking for material which I could later work on with the actors during the designated devising periods. Programmes about the slave trade, the rise of black power in the USA, and urban slum clearance. In addition (and inspired by the local documentary plays mounted by Peter Cheeseman and his company at the nearby Victoria Theatre Stoke-on-Trent) we researched and performed a series of plays on the car industry, Coventry's major employer.

Then an actor recently returned from an RSC tour to Japan gave me a newspaper article which was, in effect, the last will and testament of a nine year old Japanese girl from a small fishing town called Minamata. Before Ioka died (horribly) of mercury poisoning caused by the release of poisoned industrial effluent into Minamata Bay, she had been interviewed by a local radio reporter. She movingly asked that the cause of her death should not be forgotten. The Chisso Factory had always denied that its outflow pipes were the reason that the fish, and then the sea birds, and then the children were dying in grotesque spasms. Ioka called for a worldwide movement to fight what she called 'the Minamata war' – in effect a war against pollution. It was a plea to which, I felt, we could not fail to respond! This was in 1973 – before the environmental movement had made any significant impact.

Further research threw up a Japanese documentary film with footage of the very sick Ioka, and of parents and grandparents who had had to nurse young victims of the mercury poisoning. We immediately felt that their own words should be, wherever possible, the bedrock of the play.

> **Grandparent**: I have three grandchildren with the disease; Myseo, Alika and Marsaki. Marsaki is a very severe case. He is totally deaf and dumb. I've seen children with the disease play with healthy children and the parents of the healthy children drag their children away. They spank them for playing with our children. I've seen it with my own eyes! Can you believe such things could happen?

The film also showed the efforts of the fishermen to gain compensation from the company. Ignored, the impoverished fishermen told their story (often to smartly-dressed beneficiaries of the 'Japanese economic miracle' of which the Chisso Company was a part). A supporter told the fisherman that if each of them owned a single share in the Chisso Company they would be allowed into its Annual General Meeting in Tokyo. This could get their campaign nationwide publicity. 'The one-share-movement' was born. At the AGM the victims held up photos of their dead children. They invited the Chisso executives to drink from a bucket of water taken from Minimata Bay – water the company claimed was unpolluted. The executives declined to drink the water. The image of the politely smiling executives faced by photo after photo in black-edged frames of the dead children went round the world. It was to become the final image of the play.

The Pursuit of Justice

Drink the Mercury!: This was to be a play for eight to twelve year olds. In developing a play for young audiences one looks for a central child protagonist who encapsulates the political/social or historical theme you wish to explore – and this material offered that directly. The proposition to the audience is: 'You are an audience of nine, ten and eleven year olds – here is a fellow nine year old who would play like you, have friends like you, ride a bike, and a thousand and one simple things. But she was never able to do those things. And she wanted everyone to know why. So here's her story.' But what was the best way for the nine year old Ioka, now dead of course, to address these children of her own age?

I knew we should be as restrained as possible in putting the horrible events in front of the audience. So I devised a non-naturalistic structure which constantly reminds the audience they were watching a constructed 'theatre' piece. The factory was an exotic masked figure with ultra-long fingers representing the pipes which took the effluent into the sea. Ioka's cat, the first to spasm and die after feeding off fish scraps, was played by a masked actor – the death spasms brief and balletic. Each small scene of Ioka's life was brought to an end with the actors involved bowing to the audience, and creating a break before the next scene started. In the scene of Ioka's death, she haltingly speaks her final words to the visiting radio reporter. She says she would like to go on a ship and visit every continent. There she would tell the people what had happened to her and ask them to join her in fighting the Minamata War. The parents seeing her difficulty in speaking simply say to the radio man, 'No more.'

Ioka, in her parent's arms, stares ahead. A gong sounds. The actor playing Ioka rises. She takes an ornate scarf from her neck and

Ioka has lost her sight

places it on the ground. Thereafter the presence of the dead Ioka is represented by the scarf. All the actors in the scene then rise, bow to the audience and move to the side. There is another gong, and the next scene assembles round the scarf as the parents of Ioka call on the village to do what Ioka no longer can – take her plea for action to the world. I think that this austere theatre style helped the children come to terms with Ioka's story in a way that was acceptable. The other thing that convinced me we could justify playing to this age group was the central issue – the pursuit of justice. If there is one thing this age group is majorly concerned with, it is justice – or in the case of the Minamata fishermen – injustice. It was a David and Goliath story. And the Davids in this story were not just victims, they were fighters – for justice.

Dramatising Nazism

No Pasaran!: Moving in the mid-1970's to join the Octagon Theatre Company in Bolton, another town (like Coventry) with a large Asian population, it did not take long to feel the rising racial tension in the town fomented by the rise of small far-right parties. In this context, I started to prepare a play about racism and the rise of Nazism. The danger in any such 'historical' project is that the material will feel like a school lesson. Playing to an audience of fourteen to seventeen year olds is no picnic. As the performers arrive at the school their eyes deliver a wordless, but clear message. 'I'm bored now. I'll be bored by whatever you're going to show me.' It's a wonderful challenge. For a company writer it is very important because, of course, if the play does not engage the audience, it is your colleagues, the actors, who will have to perform your less than dynamic work.

I had no interest in portraying the major historical figures: I wanted to put on stage a kid, an ordinary kid of the streets, the same age as the audience – who had lived through this period. Obviously it had to be a Jewish youngster. I wanted to see him before the rise of Hitler, when he had aspirations, dreams, a future – then take him through the growing nightmare of the Germany of the Swastika. I did not assume the audience, born in the 60's, would be eager to immerse themselves in these far past days. My job was to bring this era vividly alive, to throw the audience into the progress of a life which would catch them off guard and sweep them along. An early action of Nazi law-makers had been to ban Jewish sportsmen. It was a criminal offence for 'Aryan' sportsmen to compete with or against Jews. Assimilated Jews had enjoyed a prominent position in German sport. There were Jewish football internationals and Olympic champions. But by 1933 no longer.

The action opens with two sixteen year old boxing-gloved youngsters slugging it out in a sparring session in 1932. As they throw punches, we hear German radio. The next Games have been awarded to their home town, Berlin. One of the two boxers, Jan Goldberg, is overjoyed. In four years time he will wear the German eagle. A year later, the Nazis are in power.

The play follows Jan through the nazification of German social life. Jan is expelled from his boxing club and from his school. A teacher who stands up for him and other expelled Jews, is fired. Former friends turn away from him out of fear as decrees reduce the status of Jews to that of non-persons. Our audience, including Asian and black youngsters watched this process with growing fascination – often in disbelief. The 1936 Olympics on which Jan had set his heart, finally arrives. A meeting with some British boxers leads him to being a sparring partner. They become friends, and through Jan the British boys come to realise the nature of Nazi rule, and the hopelessness of his ever being a Jewish sportsman in Germany. On their final night in Berlin he joins them to see the black American sprinter Jesse Owens, another 'sub-human' according to Hitler, win his gold medal to the wild enthusiasm of a packed stadium. Jan experiences a brief joy at seeing Hitler's 'Aryan superman' theory shown for what it is and, at the invitation of his new boxing friends, heads for England.

Giving evidence

The second half of the play shows Jan in the East End of London as Britain's Fascists bid for power by assaults on the Jewish quarter, culminating in 'The Battle of Cable Street.' Jan later returns to Germany, and is swallowed up as the world moves towards war. The final scenes of the play show one of the British boxers who has befriended Jan in Berlin (and is now a soldier) trying to trace him. As a military clerk starts the hopeless task of finding his name in a concentration camp death book, the soldier hears a Polish survivor of Auschwitz taken through the evidence she is to give to the Nuremberg Court. Potentially cynical young audiences responded to the human story.

Plays on the Third World

The Disappeared: In the early 80's, Theatre Centre commissioned a series of plays for secondary school audiences on life in the Third World. I wrote a play about the 1970's 'dirty war' in Argentina based on the experiences of 'the Mothers of the Plaza de Mayo,' the brave women who had lost sons, daughters or grandchildren as the military junta had 'disappeared' up to 30,000 civilians in a violent internal war. The play starts with a tested technique – the mothers holding photos of their disappeared youngsters, and demanding of the military junta if they were alive or dead. 'Where are the Disappeared!' The actors circle the audience briefly indicating the circumstances of these disappearances before they are violently cleared by the Argentine Army. *The Disappeared* then takes the audience through one particular story of a teacher who has been 'lifted' by a death squad as her pupils watch. The play is the story of two of these children and their remaining teacher, as they face life under the military dictatorship, a form of government which at that time dominated every Latin American State except Venezuela.

Magpie Theatre

The play was also produced by Magpie, the leading young peoples' theatre company in Australia. Adults were as shocked and moved and swept along by the drama as much as the students. I was asked to come and write another play. I readily agreed. The commission was for a play principally for eight to twelve year olds but once again adults would be a significant part of the audience. I resolved to write the play for the children and let the adults make of it what they might – a decision I would always make in such circumstances. I had no idea what the play was going to be about.

On my first night in Australia, a tremendous all-night thunder storm crashed down on the tin roof of the one-storey home to which I'd been invited. My host said, 'You've just heard five hundred million dollars on the balance of payments.' I smelt a story – who wouldn't? He told me about the year-after-year of waiting for rain, the dying animals, the bankrupted small farmers. Then – the forced migration to the city.

Research in Schools and the Community

I walked around an area of Adelaide where there were significant numbers of new migrants. I came upon a crudely daubed sign which read 'Boat People Go Home.' Clearly the outback refugees I had been thinking about had one sort of problem; the new arrivals from Vietnam another. Perhaps I could bring these two stories into the same stage ambit; two small girls moving separately towards an unknown city, one unhappily from a bankrupt farm, another from a ravaged war zone.

I headed for 'the bush'. Head teachers were phoned. I met the kids, told them I was a 'city slicker', and would they tell me about their lives. The children talked, then took me to the farm and showed me. I learned about drought and what it does. The children started to have me understand why being forced off the land into the city was such a bad prospect for them. 'The city??,' one said in horror, 'aw mister, there's nothing to do there!' And having seen them working alongside parents on the farm, driving their own trucks and tractors with large wooden blocks added so they could reach the pedals, I began to understand what they meant. I then returned to the city via Melbourne, gathering material on the Vietnamese migrants.

What made me think I could write a play about Australia after a six week visit? I called the play *No Worries* – an expression I had heard everywhere up-country.

Telling Untold Tales

The play opened. I had written the scenes within a continuing sung ballad (performed by the company). The ballad play portrays one country girl's active life as her family moves slowly towards bankruptcy and eviction during the drought. Exiled to the city, her world shattered, she retreats into a world of silence. Across from her in a city school there is another silent girl, a Vietnamese who as yet knows no English. By the end of the play they will provide a kind of salvation for each other. A Le Coq trained actor, Geoffrey Rush, directed the actors to play sheep movement and the many animals in the drama. Finally the lights came up after the dramatic ending as the two ten year old children (played by adult actors) exchange their first words, one speaking in English, the other Vietnamese. I looked around and many of the adults in the audience were in tears.

One sought me out later. 'You've told the story of my life.' His reaction turned out to be far from unique. As the run progressed many people said so. The implication slowly dawned on me that, at least in these people's view, nobody else had told this story. Soon the play was being produced round the country, Melbourne, Brisbane, Sydney and Perth to similar reactions. A year later, the play was a set book on the national literature syllabus, and I was being called an Australian writer (and the film that was made from it represented Australia at Film Festivals). I didn't argue.

Socially-aware and Internationalist Theatre

What I learnt from working in TIE was the capability of involving a young audience in socially-aware theatre, and not playing down to them. Young audiences need socially-aware theatre in the current age of globalisation. One can detect a continuum in mainstream British theatre with the re-emergence of documentary plays in fringe venues – on the murder of the black teenager Stephen Lawrence, the Hutton Enquiry on the war in Iraq and on a larger scale, the 'verbatim' plays by David Hare at the National Theatre.

Through these years I have, along with many others, carried the torch for a theatre for the young which is both socially-aware and internationalist, but also exciting and emotionally involving. I would not like a play of mine to take its young audience to a 'never never land', but rather to a faraway place where children's lives are very different – probably much shorter and more hazardous than their own – and by means of the theatre, bring them together.

David Holman has written key plays for leading companies in the UK, Australia and across the world.

THEATRE CENTRE AND NEW WRITING

Rosamunde Hutt on how Theatre Centre commissions plays on contemporary themes, and develops new writers.

Snapshot of Theatre Centre – 1993 to 2004

Small Miracles: A theatre academic professor described our plays to me as 'small miracles' – 32 commissioned and toured nationwide to schools and theatres since 1993. 7 by first time playwrights – half by Black and Asian writers.

Dramaturgy: Developed with our audiences, a process now imitated elsewhere. The content of the work engages with contemporary themes and its contemporary audience.

Community development: *Authentic Voices* project in which nine young writers from London's East End collaborate on a play, *Reality Check*, performed professionally.

Renewing the Vision

Theatre Centre's 40th Anniversary in 1993. I speak with founder, Brian Way, pioneer of theatre for young people. 'Theatre Centre's concern – opening the doors and windows of the heart, mind and spirit. The fundamental experience of theatre should be one of intuitive understanding through emotional involvement, not of intellectual comprehension, through novel ways of imparting facts.' I work to Brian's image of 'opening doors and windows' to articulate the company's vision – to imagination, to understanding, to utopias and to creativity.

How to express this vision in action? The Theatre Centre team, Associate Artists, Nettie Scriven, and myself take stock of our legacy – the development of children's dramatists under the direction of Brian Way's successors, David Johnston and Libby Mason. The guiding principles established were :

- the cultural diversity of a multi-ethnic society for its young audiences

- equal opportunities in its artistic practice through, for example, integrated casting
- scenography as a formative dimension of its production process

Seminal Workshop

We set up a Company Workshop to reflect on the past and identify narratives for the future. A writer depicts her son as a parcel tied to a chair, her theme 'the young black British man without hope – a personal response as a black mother – a professional response as a theatre practitioner.' This image was formative, and influenced later Theatre Centre work. This seminal workshop resulted in a newly-minted Artistic Policy, which set out the landscape we wanted to explore.

Three Cycles : Rites of Passage, Exploration of Contemporary Culture, Releasing the Authentic Voice

Seven Themes :
- Childhood in a world made by adults
- Roots, belonging, home
- Exclusion, difference, identity, diversity, commonalities, shared humanity
- Violence, fear, mean streets, privilege, consumerism
- Men, women, love, the family, relationships
- Creativity, release, possibility
- The cycle of life, birth, death

We had set out our stall. A Board member responded: 'Through your work you make material accessible, to help people to think and make comparisons. The point of theatre is to take the audience into imaginative worlds and conceptualize things.'

Sensitive issues

The first play I directed for Theatre Centre was *Turncoat* by Diane Samuels. Two women fall in love. These were the days of Section 28, a law that forbade the 'promotion' of homosexuality in schools. The Board stood at my side. This was business as usual, Theatre Centre taking risks. Ten years on and we've broken the rules, stormed the schools with big gestures and bold ideas, with shows that continue to set off alarm bells. In our 50th year, we presented Rosy Fordham's

Missing, one of the most courageous plays we've done, presenting the story of a girl who goes missing and does not return. People are nervous about this show, teachers cancel and we use gentle persistence and in-depth teachers' resource packs to woo them back on board. We no longer have to defend our stand; we aim to work in partnership. Whether it is the fear of the unknown (*Under The Bed*), or family violence (*Listen to your Parents*), we specialise in enabling sensitive issues to be presented.

Working with writers

We talk. They bring ideas. Or we take them to a school. I always ask: 'What are you passionate about?' Sometimes we circle round. Sometimes it is absolutely clear what will work. We discover our writers through networking. It is important that the writers care about our audiences. But it is central that we enable our writers to write from the heart, not fitting into a preconceived set of givens. We are interested in those under-represented in the theatre industry. We commit ourselves to writers, very few write just one piece for us. Leading playwrights also knock on our door with new ideas. We are writer-centred, trying to find the best method for each individual. To create a canon of good quality dramatic work the creativity of the writers has to be released. Paradoxically, the Thematic Cycle approach has in

Neil Greig with two new writers

practice anchored the project, and ensured relevance to the young peoples' audience.

The Process in Action: November 2002 – dramaturge, experienced writer, Noël Greig, and I sit with new writer, Manjinder Virk. A process starts. First draft. Her first draft gently touches on sensitive issues: an Asian girl/white boy relationship, loss, and her father's experience as an immigrant. Manjinder talks about Mohammad Ali, as does Kul, the character she is creating. Noël: 'you are both passionate about him. He's waiting in the wings – bring him on!' Next draft. Mohammad Ali arrives to Kul in a vision. Her anger at being called a Paki (a Pakistani), and Ali's rage at the racism he experienced bounces off the set. *Glow* – as the play becomes called – now encompasses the epic, as well as the personal.

Theatre Centre Plays

Inclusive audience experience: In our individualist, mobile-phone texting, digital age we have a commitment to create an inclusive shared experience. The show must engage the least experienced, and the most sophisticated audience members. Writers approach this in different ways, using direct address (*Positive Mental Attitude*), very contemporary use of language (*Look At Me*), references to modern culture (*Gorgeous*). Other productions attract because they hit the zeitgeist (*Missing*), or through powerful sustained interaction between characters like Chekhov (*Souls*).

Form and theatricality: Whilst developing a play we are not only looking at the word, but also at image-making, visual narrative and music. Within the rigours of touring, we focus on composition and choreography, believing that the physical spatial relationships enhance the meaning of the play. We create intimate performance spaces where you can hear the actor breathing near you, you can feel the decisions being made, and you can see the detail on the shoe.

A teacher challenged us in 2000. 'Our pupils love your 'other worlds' shows – not your teenage-based pieces'. We decide to keep offering both to our audiences, and sharpen up our vision in action. Our 'other worlds' repertoire looks at universal themes, bearing witness to events on the world's stage. Our 'here and now' repertoire looks at what it is like to be alive and young in the twenty-first century.

What have I learned as a Director?

Get one-hour play action started straight away: You can't warm up for twenty minutes. A writer steeped in the world of the audience, five to fifteen years old, can produce material that will speak both to the child and the teacher. Never patronise or underestimate – subtlety works. Dramaturge Bryony Lavery asks each writer – what is your gift to the audience? We try to show life as it is, but as the plays are for young people we often conclude with images of possibility e.g. an open door, the cry of a new born baby, a game of chase, a dance of reconciliation, or a bold statement of defiance.

Black and Asian writing is a necessity: The stories are shouting to be heard. Huge themes are being explored by writers such as Angela Turvey who says of writing *Precious*, 'as a young black woman, she is living out the personal and emotional consequences of recent history – post-war immigration to Britain, colonialism, and, ultimately, slavery'.

Releasing the Authentic Voice: This cycle has resulted in a body of work that deeply affects our audiences. In some places, the impact is audiences identifying with the characters: 'our pupils found the Asian actors and content inspiring' (*Skin Into Rainbows*). In others, it is presenting worlds with which they are unfamiliar: 'our area is very mono-cultural. I felt they took note of many unquantifiable aspects which subtly made them think' (*A Fine Example*).

Apparently hostile audience: Their jeers, whispered comments and impulsive roars can shake an actor used to the studio space, but in fact their heckles remind us that theatre can be a boxing ring, a debating chamber (even if it feels like the Coliseum at times).

Issue-based Theatre: Sometimes British YPT theatre is criticised for being too issue-based or didactic. In fact the in-depth rigorous approach from our Theatre-in-Education heritage, married with contemporary theatre-making techniques, can lead to a piece of theatre that is both educationally rooted and a high example of theatrical craft.

Be organic – not mechanistic: You need then to be able to break the rules – one writer needs to go abroad for their research, another wants to talk to small groups of pupils, he wants to hear what everyone thinks, she wants the world to read her very first draft, this script is Top Secret, 'only for the eyes of Rosamunde'.

Know when to intervene: And when intervention becomes interference. You can dramaturge a piece too much so that the bite and originality that grabbed you all in the first place withers and dies. But crucially you *have* to voice your doubts. A mistake lives with you for always. A shared vision of process and how to deliver is vital. When the chips are down it is rehearsal time, personnel, resources that come under threat, all the ingredients for quality work. It takes a lot of nerve.

'Collective' to 'Collaborative' Practice

I myself started in an actors' collective (Spectacle Theatre), with all decisions collective (even what colour to paint the van), went on to directing with a co-operative (Hijinx Theatre), creating devised theatre through improvisation, collaborating with writers. Then I moved as Artistic Director to Theatre Centre, where all the writers and performers are freelance.

We have rehearsed readings of each new play with the Theatre Centre staff and Associate Artists, and ask – what are the striking images? What for you is the heart/essence of the play? Are there any questions that you would like to ask the writer? Do you identify with the themes and characters? Is there anything here which reflects your own life or the lives of the people that you know?

We have sessions in schools on ideas and early drafts of the play. These allow us to share our methodologies and knowledge with teachers and with pupils. In return we hear their voices, which sharpen our understanding of their worlds. We check: do the young people understand the story? How does that influence character development or use of language? Has every element of the play a strong dramatic function?

We document the impact of the piece on students, teachers and artists. Who laughs? Who cries? Who looks perplexed, and why? And we tease out the subtleties. A typical interrogation with pupils might be:

Two actors play a scene. Director stops at a key moment of change. Asks questions:

- what's at stake here? who wants what?
- what is the story of this scene? what do we know?
- what does she need? want?

- how has the character moved on at the end of the scene?
- what is their status? when does it change? who's winning?
- what can we tell from their physicality? who is open? closed?
- what might the character be thinking? is it the same as she is saying?
- what made an impact on you from the text?

We try out the material in schools. At a failing school we play a scene from the first draft of Noël Greig's *Trashed*. A young man in his twenties tells his mother that he is gay.

> **Louisa:** And here is something else, my boy – it's against God.
> **Mel:** Now that is taking it too far.
> **Louisa:** I know my bible.
> **Mel:** Jesus hung out with twelve guys!
> **Louisa:** And I have a line son, a line when it comes to what's right and what is wrong.

I ask the pupils (aged fourteen and fifteen) their responses. Some are 'cool' about it, others horrified. One student volunteers to play the young man in role. The teenagers laugh and rub their hands in glee. The teacher looks nervous. An improvisation of remarkable quality takes place. We are stunned, so is the teacher.

Follow-up activities to a performance of *Precious* by Angela Turvey.

I look at responses.

– A pupil writes: "Precious was tied down by her family, her age and a baby. She was not the type to sit back and watch her life pass without achieving her goals. I think she represented her cultural background and her longing to be free."
– A student performs an improvised monologue as Precious: "I sit in the chair, centre stage with my shoulders close together. My hands on my belly where the Baby would be. I could link my feelings for Precious to the way she felt in the play, trapped and isolated."

These follow-up activities reveal what we want to achieve through the plays commissioned by and toured by Theatre Centre – empowering the young audiences to look at social, political, visual, symbolic, and cultural issues.

Looking for the next generation

Although a play is initially the idea of one single person, its fruition is the gift of the young people who engage with the play's development, the artists who bring the production to life, the administrators who manage the play, and the audience who provides their responses. Beyond this lies the field, our YPT colleagues, and the domain, which is, or is not forever changed. At the end of all this collaboration my role as Director is actually a magpie, a midwife, a facilitator. There is nothing if there are not great ideas, there is no play without the artistic impulse of one mind, the first conversation where a writer says 'I have got the idea that ... ' Hence our search for the next generation of writers who will make work for tomorrow's audiences, writers that will create the next set of 'small miracles', small in scale maybe, but big, bold and beautiful in terms of artistic ambition, and contemporary relevance for our audiences.

SIX PLAYS FOR YOUNG AUDIENCES

Thomas Kell on why Theatre Centre has published plays it has commissioned and successfully toured, and gives an insight into six plays in their Anthology.

Why we started publishing scripts

Theatre Centre lavishes time and resources upon the development of its new plays, but where does our work go then? Fine plays 'disappear', partly because they are not sitting on a shelf in the bookshops, easily available to students and teachers.

To date Theatre Centre has published *Little Violet and the Angel* by Philip Osment (Oberon) and seen *Jumping on My Shadow* published by Faber in its Anthology. With Aurora Metro we have released Leo Butler's *Devotion* (young people in a war zone), Charles Way's, *A Spell of Cold Weather* and Noël Greig's *Trashed*, (sexual identity), and have also published our *Anthology of Plays for Young People* published in 2003, one of the highpoints of our 50th Anniversary year.

Listen to Your Parents by Benjamin Zephaniah

Mark listens. He is a teenage football-fan, a writer of poetry – and a witness. His mother is receiving a terrible beating tonight. By his father. He is used to seeing her face purpled with bruises. What she looks like now he can't imagine. Words pour out, trying to cover the noise.

> **Mark:** Sometimes, I just don't care about you and your wars. Sometimes I just don't care about you. Sometimes I just want to beat the pain up. And kill the pressure. Sometimes I just want to go and scream in church. Then fly home to make my very own Dad.'

Benjamin Zephaniah is passionately committed to young people, the holder of strong political convictions, and a man whose pores pour poetry. *Listen to Your Parents* began as a BBC Radio Play. Nottingham Round-about in partnership with Theatre Centre, brought it to the stage. The play is an uncompromising portrayal of domestic violence; not just that inflicted upon a wife by her husband, but the impact of that violence on a teenage boy, Mark. The violence itself is brutal; the dialogue between parents suffused with constant menace. In contrast poetry bursts out of Mark, about football, about Maria, the love of his life, about his threatened family.

Listen to your Parents

Mark's family is from Jamaica. His best friend, Wali, is a refugee from Afghanistan who carries his past with boyish lightness. Mark yearns for normality, struggling to comprehend that Wali's father doesn't hit his wife. Zephaniah's writing posits constructs of 'home', evoked by Mark's poetry.

> **Mark:** The damp hangs around the bathroom. Lingers in the kitchen. And watches o'er us like a dark menacing cloud. Jamaica must be here somewhere. Coconuts and cashew nuts cook themselves. And the aunties and the uncles. Walk like they have springs in their feet. And drums on their minds. Is this Jamaica?

The play structure is a week which will end in a trial for Mark with Aston Villa. There is a religious dimension; 'creationism' in his father's terms, presents man supreme over all life, including woman. Mark's week is a progression towards an unexpected act of violence which ends, for the moment – all hope. *Listen to Your Parents* presents a bleak vision ultimately, and a stirring call to confront domestic violence ('real terrorism' in Zephaniah's words), but one illuminated by youthful optimism and vibrant, glowing poetry.

Precious by Angela Turvey
The play opens with Precious, a black British teenager, on a nocturnal graffiti spree.

> **Precious:** Everyone knows me, 'See her, she'll come to nothing – end up wasting her life.' That's what they want, the self-fulfilling prophecy – becoming what they say I am – a waster, a vandal. But I don't destroy anything. I just make my mark.

Precious brings new colours to immaculate, whitewashed walls. School, exams, jobs – the real world – intrude. She dreams of escape, of living somewhere else with her best friend Kamala (Asian British).

> **Precious:** Somewhere where we would just blend in.
> **Kamala:** You never actually do anything do you Precious... you criticise my life and you're just stuck here doing nothing. You don't even know what you want.

There is a way out for Kamala: an arranged marriage to a family friend in Florida. A shadow falls over the girls' friendship. Woman, an enigmatic character from the future, enters Precious' life, assigned as a mentor. She is a proper artist. Art brings them together, then they are united by opposing fortunes. 'Woman cannot have a child: I will never experience that love, the love of a mother for her child. The sky is ice blue and a weak, faded sun gives no warmth.' Precious becomes pregnant, but her determination to be an artist is overwhelming. A child has no place in her plan. She aborts it. A terrible choice, rejecting the potential to belong 'to my body, to other women.' Woman thinks back to her first love, twenty years ago. A kind of fission occurs: Precious and Woman morph into the future. Then Kamala and Precious meet again at an exhibition of Precious' work. She is now a successful artist. Kamala's life has turned out fine. They dance as they did in their youth.

We wondered whether the YPT movement is ready for this play, its characters, and their simmering anger and dissatisfaction. We hope our plays will be taken on by other companies, Precious offers a complex presentation of generational conflict, and eventual rapprochement.

Look at Me by Anna Reynolds

All the clocks in Kandi and Nick's lives are ticking down. Exclusion. Expulsion. Out. They exhaust all the meagre capacity for care that can be offered by school, social workers, family. Yet in each other they find connection. And tonight is the first date; a night of nerves and peculiar ecstasy.

> **Nick:** We were just walking round town all night, shivering. It's still warm out. I don't dare touch her in case I let her know how scared I am. Her eyes are lit up like fireworks. Is she on something? She could be anything. She could be anyone. I don't care.

The theatrical structure is complex. Stacey has caused havoc in her mother's life, but is travelling to rapprochement with her. She has a child by her boyfriend, Moose. She arrives, magically, in the life of Kandi, who wants someone to listen to her. Now she has Stacey, who – like a malignant fairy godmother – can rewind time, can give the opportunity to un-say, un-punch, un-react. Stacey has arrived just in time. Kandi is now out of control. She doesn't know herself why she does what she does. She fights a caretaker. The Headteacher is minded to expel her for three days.

> **Kandi:** Back to before my mum got ill. I'd stop it. I'd run away then, never have to – see it, or I'd make my Dad stay, I'd watch him every minute to make sure he didn't give in and leave us with nothing, and nobody who gives a toss about us that's where I'd go!'

Stacey rewinds time for Kandi, and asks to be set free herself. Kandi is being given what she has never been aware she has, control over her own life. Nick leaves and the scene is replayed. We're not sure Kandi is going to get out of this one, that she has broken out of type. She has a vision of being something more attractive – a sense that happiness could be found.

Anna Reynolds has a unique voice; she is a poet of lives lived under the flickering neon of small town high streets. *Look at Me* is a hard play, telling us that we will repeat our mistakes. Teenage audiences responded to the wit, the challenge of unpicking the interlocking time-frames, and the exposure of dreadful choices. The play is warm, human and comic in the most Shakespearean sense.

Gorgeous by Anna Furse
Performed as a monologue, *Gorgeous* begins in the nineteenth century in the character of Victorian Alice, floating on a sea of euphemism and confusion. Already the focus of many rules and expectations, she experiences a fantastic menstruation, during which she contacts her modern self. Modern Alice soon converts her shocked forebear to the delights of contemporary teenage life: mobiles, *Macdonald's*, make-up, pick-up bras, boys. The societal and gender pressure weighing upon nineteenth century Alice is as nothing compared to that thrusting upon her more seemingly liberated sister.

> **Alice:** I can't any more! I collapse in the street, faint at school... I've shrivelled to a crisp. I'm dry as a twig. I could snap at any moment. I stink. I stink of my disappearing act...

Her self-obsession is broken by the voices of the famous symbol of perfection, Barbie. The plays grows into a world where Alice's outlook is so skewed that no objective voice can be heard, where the only reality is her body. Clearly Alice is ill. Ultimately she desires to remodel herself not through control of food intake but by a cutting, reshaping knife.

> **Alice:** Savour the moment I mark my own flesh, press ink and metal into it, inscribe it with my own story. I want to own my own body. ... And I want to emerge from my ordeal, proud of my endurance. A terrible beauty. The beauty of my power, the power of suffering... I want to be a saint. An angel!

The rescuing voice of Alice's Mother is heard, calling her back. We return to the dressing table a century before. Furse's equivocal final scene has Alice responding to the mother's summons with the words, 'Just... getting ready...' The requirements for girls to 'perform' – to make up, to dress up – but not to act up – are clear. There is the possibility of pleasure, and the play abounds in the fun of growing into adulthood, the delight and solidarity to be found in shared experience.

Glow by Manjinder Virk

Kulwinder has won a medal. She is the Champion Girl Boxer! She is just getting to know who she is. Ant, the boy with whom she had that 'moment', her personal punch bag – he's off to see *The Lord of the Rings* again. She tells him he should have her medal.

Ant: What?
Kulwinder: It's yours.
Ant: But you won it.
Kulwinder: Yeah, but you're my lucky hobbit, ain't ya!

Her inspiration is Mohammed Ali – her bedroom a shrine to his achievements. The great boxer appears as a vision, a ghost from the television so important in Kul's life outside the boxing ring. Ant's lack of ambition contrasts with Kul's fierce drive.

Kul's father, Raj has never come to terms with death of his wife; this country offers him nothing. He is at a loss for what to do with

Glow

his boxer daughter. The actor playing her father, doubles as Mohammed Ali – Kul is being offered two alternative concepts of father. Kul's journey is a journey into self-sufficiency, and puberty. She needs her mother. The evening before her big fight she wraps herself in her mother's best sari. Raj cannot accept this. Kul is violating her mother's memory. Kul wins the right to remember her mother, and evoke her presence. Boxing is Kul's way of asserting identity. Kul and her father are both struggling with their identities as British Asians.

> **Raj:** This world is not designed to help our people, understand? We made this country a success, they made us failures.

Kulwinder voices the perspective of the assimilated second generation. Her life is full of shared culture; mainstream films and television.

> **Kulwinder:** 'This is my home, this is where I was born'.

She is struggling to cope with her teenage changing body. Does her desire to box denude her femininity? Ant is likewise uneasy with his physicality, identifying with those awkward characters of the Ring. Kul steps out of Mohammed Ali's shadow, and asserts her own self. Raj witnesses her victory. Her greatest prize is his pride.

We wanted to present Virk's writing – the fresh voice of a new generation of British Asians, aware of the resentments of previous generations, and within contemporary British society, yet positively forging new possibilities and personal journeys.

Souls by Roy Williams

Roy Williams was carving out a reputation as the unofficial poet-laureate of West London street culture. Committed to young people, would Williams write for the company? He would. *Souls* sparkles like a malevolent gem in the collection. Every line seems a punch or counter-punch. There is comedy and fallibility. The key theme is men's inability to communicate adequately with one another.

Errant brother Stephen has returned home for his mother's funeral. Younger brother, Anthoney, is in awe of him, and older brother Alex still full of antagonism. Stephen has done a spell in prison. There is another character in the living room – the recently deceased mother whose things lie all over the floor, ready to be packed away by her sons, a job which Anthoney feels is disproportionately his. Her Jamaican voice sounds through the post-it sticker notes attached to backs of chairs.

Alex (*reads a sticker*): 'Alex, mek sure yu pack away all of my tings after de funeral.'

Anthoney: Yeah. 'Alex make sure.' Not – Alex make sure Anthoney does it. Bloody hell man.

Alex (*reads another sticker*): 'Anthoney! Do not swear.'

Anthoney: Piss off.

Alex (*reads another*): 'I mean it young man.'

Anthoney: Yer dry, Alex.

Alex (*shows him the sticker*): Ain't me little brother, it's Mum.

Mum is in the furniture; she is in the codes of behaviour the men struggle to implement as they turn in on themselves. Alex has problems. His vehicle repair garage is going under. Alex gets Stephen to agree to start a fire at his garage allowing him to claim the insurance. Stephen enrols Anthoney in the arson job, much to Alex's anger.

Alex: What kinda guy lets his brother do that? ... But there's gotta be a part of yu – bitta Mum tellin yu it's wrong.

Stephen and Anthoney set fire to Alex's garage but are seen. The police are due. Alex and Stephen have a final, dreadful confrontation.

Alex: Yu can't do nuttin right, all yer life. Come juss like Dad.

The brothers are reunited at the house. Even now they won't talk properly, they are relations who won't relate.

Anthoney: Thass all we do, ennit? Shut up. We don't say nuttin.

Williams dedicates his play to three generations of Black Britons: the first immigrants; Roy's generation – and the next generation. It is asking modern Black British youth in particular: what comes next as the parental generation die? Williams' characters flounder in the face of these questions. Our teenage audiences enjoyed the brothers' constant childlike fighting, which Williams turns from comedy to tragedy in an instant.

It is a core aim at Theatre Centre that we seek writing which contains the universal in the specific. Three Black British West London brothers, inhabiting a specific culture. But they could be any brothers, any siblings. Michael Judge (Associate Artist, Education) transposed the piece to local schools in Tower Hamlets where the brothers became Bangladeshi, challenging each other, and fighting for status. Human commonality filtered through cultural specificity came into focus.

Publishing Policy

We do not publish as a matter of course – only when our publisher can be persuaded of the artistic and commercial rationale. Are all new plays ready to be published? Or are we, in the general climate where first production is likely to be the last, behaving in a manner inimical to the creation of great theatrical work by fixing texts too soon? Such are the considerations crossing the mind as proofs are finally and reluctantly agreed and presses roll. The Anthology proves Theatre Centre's seriousness of intent, and belief in the quality of what we are presenting. Strange how the ephemeral nature of theatre solidifies when poured into paper and ink.

These plays are now there. We are ready for responses, for criticism, for debate. As Rosamunde Hutt writes in her introduction: "Use the volume, Make notes. Annotate, quibble, comment. A decade's work is in your hands."

Rosamunde Hutt is Director, Thomas Kell Administrator of Theatre Centre.

5. CREATING AND ADAPTING MATERIAL FOR PERFORMANCE

TRAVELLING LIGHT – Making a Play with and for Children

Jude Merrill and Cath Greig review the company's creative process.

Travelling Light is one of the few companies making and touring theatre for young people in the South West of England. We started in 1984 and are based in Bristol where we began. Our early touring circuit took us into schools in and around the Bristol area. This expanded to include theatre venues. Now school visits are out-numbered by public performances, but school parties still make up a large proportion of our audiences. We remain committed to the equal access that school visits and school parties provide. In addition, our educational experience, and knowledge of how schools operate, their needs and concerns, has proved a sound basis for our artistic development.

We aim to tour two productions a year, one new and a re-tour of a previously successful show, targeting different age groups. On average around 20,000 people a year see or participate in our work. Tours now begin in schools local to Bristol, and move on to theatres and arts centres throughout the UK. We also tour on the international circuit, with visits in recent years to Poland, Slovakia, France, Italy, the Netherlands, Canada and USA. The company is run by a core team. For each new production we put together a creative team of associate artists. Performers then work with the creative team to bring the production to life. We receive revenue funding from Arts Council (South West), Bristol City and South Gloucestershire Councils, and national touring grants from the Arts Council. We also receive local funding for our Youth Theatre.

We want our work to excite, inspire and involve young audiences – and, importantly, the adults who book the shows and buy the tickets. We do this by fusing physical energy, live music and visual imagery to create shows that draw people into the theatre experience. Underpinning all our work is the desire to create theatre of the highest possible quality. Our roots began in education, and we continue to have a commitment to providing educational activities which enriches young people's experience of our shows. We have identified two key factors influencing the quality of our theatre and education work.

1. The extended process of production. We have identified a cyclical model, in which the work undergoes research and development involving a number of artists. Exciting ideas honed until we are ready to create a new show.
2. The integration of the educational research and development process. This enables young people to become involved with the early processes of creation. As well as impacting on the show itself, it is essential to prepare the young audiences, and enhance their theatrical experience.

What we aim to achieve with every production is:

- high quality theatre for both children (or young people) and adults.
- seamless integration of many different theatrical elements
- a piece that will perform equally well in school halls, and theatre venues

The Production Process at Work

Cloudland was the first show we made that was able to undergo the whole developmental process. We wanted to make a performance for young children and their families. Our previous piece *Walking the Tightrope* was for children aged five and over. *Cloudland* was the ideal opportunity to try and discover which elements create a good quality piece of theatre to engage three and four year olds without patronising them, or resorting to slap-stick and other crowd pleasers. Our starting point was the picture book *Cloudland* by John Burningham.

A small boy, Albert, and his Mum and Dad, are enjoying a day out walking in the mountains, high above the clouds. Suddenly Albert slips and falls off a cliff. But luckily the children who live in the clouds catch him, and take him to live with them in Cloudland. The children teach Albert all sorts of lovely games to play in the clouds; jumping and racing, swimming in the rain, and dancing in the storms. When they are tired they all pile into a cloud bed and sleep. Eventually Albert becomes homesick. The Queen of Cloudland is consulted, and she promises to ask the wind to get him safely back home. Albert is very happy to find himself back again with his parents, but often thinks longingly of the time he spent up in the clouds.

Research and Try-out Period. Director, designer, music director and three actors – their task to put the book on stage in five days, using whatever means needed. The end-of-week performance to a small audience of varying ages, (who were enthusiastic, if sometimes a little bemused) was video-ed. The responses during and following the performance were carefully noted. Music and characterisation scored highly, but Sally Cookson, the director, felt the piece was too earthbound. She began to develop the idea of introducing puppets to create a truly airy feel.

We had the funding to run a series of residencies in schools. We designed a project for nursery and reception classes, using all the

Children play in *Cloudland*

Cloudland creative team. In the first residency, the designer involved the children in creating a cloudy environment. This then formed an integral part of the work in the next two schools, where puppetry and music ideas were tried out. Sally recorded her observations at all three residencies, and follow-up evaluation sessions were held with children, teachers and artists involved in the process.

The net results were:

- The artists had a much better sense of who their target audience were, and what elements of the work most engaged them.

- The children were completely enthralled by the Albert puppet and totally accepted him as one of their group. This convinced Sally that she could interchange actors and puppets with no loss of belief in their characters.
- The education team were inspired by ideas to help them plan the programme of workshops and resources to accompany the show. They decided to use the puppet Albert to introduce the story to the children during pre-show workshops, and the children's enthusiasm for music encouraged them to incorporate this as well.

Production: After analysing all our research on *Cloudland*, we finally went into rehearsals, and created a very physical performance which doesn't rely on text, but tells the story through action, music, design, dance and puppetry.

The puppets are used sparingly but to good effect. All the child characters in the play have a puppet self which enables them to operate in the air in a way that actors alone could not.

- a spinning puppet portrays Albert's fall from the mountain: the actor Albert is caught in a balletic dance by the other actors
- the puppets perform high jumps, cloud races, and Albert walking on the slipstream of a passing airplane
- the actors playing children swim in the storm clouds, have rainbow paint fights, and a jolly farewell tea party.

Set Design: To conjure up the world of the cloud children as well as the 'real' world was a challenge. The final decision was to keep it very simple. The actors create the set from a collection of bags and stepladders as they perform. The angular steps contrast with the softness of cushions, netting and cloth.

One of the ladders elevates Albert's family as they climb up the mountain. Later in the play it is used, together with swathes of material, to create an imposing and very tall Queen. When the cloud children make a bed for Albert, the audience witness how they lovingly build it from a ladder, soft material and cushions.

Lighting: A huge impact, as when the mainly blue and white set is flooded with pink light at sunset, or when Albert is swept down to earth amid a shower of sparkling lights reflected from a mirror ball.

Music: An essential element binding the whole piece together. With little text there is room for music throughout, creating atmosphere and sound effects – the wind in the mountains, the eerie boings as the children jump high in the soft bouncy clouds, the magical chimes as they pluck their breakfasts from the air, and the thunderstorm, with actors stamping and dancing and playing loud percussive instruments. Albert has a soft refrain that the children sing as they rescue him and build his cloudy bed and which returns when he is back on earth. The Man in the Moon sings a cheerful farewell to Albert as he prepares to leave Cloudland.

Storyline: The play works really well in engaging even very young children in the events of the narrative.

– Albert is an only child and it is obvious from the interaction with his parents that he is part of a close-knit family. When he falls off the mountain, instead of dwelling on this tragic event, we see him entering a completely different world, making new friends and learning new games.

– His slight clumsiness and ineptness by comparison with the 'light as bubble' cloud children gives him a vulnerability which directly relates to the young children watching it. They are all having similar experiences as they make their way in the world, and begin to grow up. Despite all the fun he is having he also suffers from homesickness, something most nursery children clearly identify with. Even though he is having a lovely time in the clouds, he misses his mother and father.

The final set

– But when the time comes to part from his new friends there is a moment of great poignancy, which causes some children to weep in sympathy, and in memory of the times when they too had to leave a lovely place, or a favourite game. Albert's happiness at finding his parents again is overshadowed by what he is missing, a common experience for children and adults alike.

Evaluation: Feedback about *Cloudland*, was gathered by follow up calls with theatre programmers and marketing departments/questionnaires completed by teachers/comments book for older audience members/feedback sheets for children. In addition we received unsolicited drawings, letters and emails from children and adults.

"I like the big cloud and everyone sleeping. I love the little puppets." **Abigail, 4**

"I would like to live in the clouds." **Paul, 8**

"I liked the shiny ball that made lights in the sky. I want to come again." **Ella, 3** – "and so do I!" **Nana, 3**

"Rainbow-paint fights are now part of our daily routine!" **Parents**

"Now we're all buzzing with ideas for creative follow-up." **Whitchurch Primary School**

"I'm sure every performance creates a new generation of future theatre-goers." **Parent**

We learned how to pitch the performance to engage the youngest members. There's no guaranteed recipe, but the following ingredients are all useful:

- Close proximity to the audience helps young children engage with the performance. *Cloudland* had less impact in the prosc-arch Royal Lyceum Theatre than in the small studios and school halls
- Direct contact with the actors at key moments creates a bond with children which helps draw them into the story
- Puppets work well for the smallest children, and charm adults
- Playing around with scale and perspective, as we did with the ladders and the puppets, is fascinating for young children who are beginning to look outward from their own small universe into a gigantic world
- Music is a vital link with very young, and therefore less verbal, children, and those with little English

- Children and adults are enchanted by magic and moments which linger in the mind long after the performance has finished
- Choosing a team familiar with the age group is essential

Sally Cookson: 'What I learnt from *Cloudland* more than anything else is that young audiences respond very honestly to theatre. They don't disguise their feelings. If they are bored they will fidget and talk and want to leave. If they are frightened they will cry. If they find something funny they will laugh, and if they are engaged in the storytelling they will watch attentively.'

To tell a story well in theatre, whether it is a story for adults, children or both, it is important to leave space for people to interpret the images offered. It can be tempting to fill each moment on stage with high energy action and masses of information.But children can delight in the most subtle story telling if done with integrity and truth. The moment in *Cloudland* when Albert sits alone missing his mum and dad had much more resonance for me because it had very few words, very little physical action, beautiful singing and a strong emotion. Simplicity and clarity were two words I found myself repeating a lot during the rehearsal period, and I think they are key to making good theatre, not just for young people but for everyone.

As a company we learned a lot about how to create appropriate and imaginative education projects for children aged three to six.

- Pre-performance workshops can engage young children in a performance before they see it, working on the premise of repetition = familiarity = confidence and acceptance
- An installation can add immeasurably to children's imaginative exploration of a story. The children were completely absorbed by the work of designing, building and playing in the Cloudland environment. Their sense of ownership was complete
- Teachers appreciate having as many resources as possible in advance of the performance in these days of forward planning, and curriculum constraints
- The cloud-bag of memories for Albert, containing a few small treasures, which was given to each school at the end of our visit, was a wonderful means of helping the children to remember key elements of the performance

Early Years Follow-up. We also learned which networks and partnerships are most useful for supporting and extending Early Years work. We became involved with a very exciting Early Years programme with five different projects over the course of a year. Our two education workers used elements of the production and installation to spark off imaginative ideas about Albert and space/time travel. A national conference at the end of the project had a special performance of *Cloudland* for the delegates. The project was so successful that we have been asked to participate again this year.

'It takes real skill and guts to produce theatre for children like this. Travelling Light remain one of the unsung heroes of theatre today.'

The Guardian

Jude Merrill, Artistic Producer, has been with Travelling Light since its early days in 1987. Cath Greig, General Manager, was a teacher before moving into arts administration.

WORKING WITH A CHILDREN'S WRITER
– a Director's Journey

Vicky Ireland recounts adapting children's books for the stage, and directing actors to perform for children.

In 1999, I decided on a journey which I'm still travelling. At that time I was Artistic Director of Polka Theatre and my most important task was to programme plays that balanced artistic integrity with box office success. I had to maintain both passion and objectivity over a long time. In order to stay relevant, I constantly sought advice about the choice of material from teachers, practitioners and children. From the children, one name kept cropping up – Jacqueline Wilson. I read her books, enjoyed them immensely and found one I liked which also had good curriculum interest.

The Lottie Project: features the everyday life and problems of a young modern girl, Charlotte, and the creation of the diary of her Victorian alto ego – Lottie. Programming this was a gamble, but the production proved to be a great success both artistically – and financially. It was the start of a working relationship between Jacqueline and myself that is ongoing. She loved the whole process of creating theatre and being part of it, attending brainstorms and workshops, and supporting the production and cast to the hilt.

With budget for six actors, I had to create the Victorian diary, which had a huge cast. I decided to film the diary like an old Victorian photo album, with video clips dispersed through the on stage action, plus narrator and silent movie piano track. And who played my many Victorians? The whole of the Polka staff, one hugely enjoyable Sunday, all carefully dressed, wigged and moustachio-ed in Victorian attire. We made our silent film and had much fun in the process.

One giant book formed the stage and another upright open book became the video screen. As the dramatic action progresses, our leading character, Charlie, writes her diary and for each chapter sits at the side of the stage as the lights dim. Once the diary clip is seen, her task is to gain the children's attention – and the dramatic flow as we move from film to live action. By dint of focused energy and sheer charisma the actress achieved this. She was passionate about the character she was playing and this sense of urgency addressed the way she communicated. You had to listen to her story.

Double Act: Five years later, Jacqueline's fame was growing. I decided to stage another book. Waiting for film and TV rights to be cleared took months but I finally managed to acquire the stage rights. A story of two funny feisty twelve year old twins. This posed my biggest challenge. I decided not to look for twins but to try to match spirits and energies, and use matching clothes and plaited wigs to create the illusion. The gods were on my side. I found two wonderfully fresh and vital young actresses who became the twins. They had a bond both on and off stage.

Action can be as eloquent as words for children and balances ear with eye. We workshopped the idea of twins, and created dance routines that mirrored their twin-ness, and their naughtiness. Within the action, I let them work out their own mannerisms. They delighted me with small, subtle details such as swinging a plait at the same time, sitting at the same time, eating in a similar manner. We spent some time on the dramatic moment when Ruby enters, having cut off her hair. This is a desperate and pathetic attempt on her behalf to stop being a twin, and become an individual. The shock and grief the other twin feels is overwhelming. The only way we found to express these feelings was through a short dance piece. Words were inadequate but movement said it all. I like this fusion.

Double Act

Bad Girls: Next the story of a timid middle-class girl who is being bullied at school and her unlikely friendship with a sassy, amoral foster child, a right bad girl. Once again I've been saved by finding inspired actresses to play young people with conviction and honesty. At the start of production, I take my cast to visit a local school so they can meet the age range they're playing and talk to the children, reacquaint themselves with young people. When we return, the actors often reproduce the behaviour they've seen, but then we work to tone this down. The challenge is not to act 'being a child', but keep the spirit inside you and let it inform your behaviour.

Here is a real range of mood – a delicate moment where Tanya tries to talk about a deeply private subject, her little sister, Carmel. Mandy is timid but also very curious. Tanya is unused to sharing her feelings but needs desperately to talk. They finish up each upsetting the other without meaning to, and then both find a way through.

Mandy: You're so lucky. Mrs Williams never nags you like my mum.

Tanya: Well that's because she's my foster mum. She doesn't really care about me. Your mum nags because she's absolutely dotty about you, anyone can see that. And your dad loves you to bits.

Mandy: What about your dad?

Tanya: Him! haven't seen him for yonks. Don't want to.

Tanya slumps

Mandy: I'm sorry.

Tanya: What for?

Mandy: I didn't mean to upset you about your dad.

Tanya: I don't give a toss about him. Or my mum, or my brothers. They've been adopted and they're doing great. It's just Carmel.

Mandy: Won't they let you see her?

Tanya: We had this supervised visit at Easter but she got all shy, her foster Mum was there and ... Look, shut up Mandy. I don't want to talk about it, OK?

Mandy: OK.

Mandy now slumps

My advice to both actresses was to feel the rhythm of the lines and honour them. They needed to be courageous to pause, to hold the moment when nothing is spoken but a lot is being felt. Trust that children can wait and listen. So often in children's theatre frenetic acting and relentless pace takes the place of truth. When pace is required this should be achieved by speeding up the thought process rather than just 'acting more quickly.' Whatever, the action needs to be lucid to keep the audience listening and buoyant to keep their attention.

Dramatising each Book

Adults are sometimes puzzled that Jacqueline Wilson holds her children readers in such thrall, but her charisma shines because she celebrates the small and major disasters and triumphs which they experience with true insight. Her characters are credible, naughty, exciting and willful.

Bad Girls

Alongside the everyday, she tackles full on difficult and disturbing facets of life that adults often won't share or discuss. She makes them accessible and lets children in on the sadnesses of life. This has a resonance for me as I want to make theatre for and with children, not at them in order to score artistic points. Often the children's plays I see are about childhood, looking back down the wrong end of the binoculars from an adult perspective, a perspective the child has yet to experience. The adults laugh, the children are confused, and I am left asking who's this for?

The process of adaptation starts with reading and re-reading the book, until – just like a burglar finding a way into a house – I can climb into the story and walk around inside it. I can hear the characters and imagine them in their everyday lives. Then I have to decide what is the story about, I mean really about? What about time? Who tells the story? Where is it placed? What about the characters? What do I cling to? Some details have to go. Others I need flag up for clarity. I can re-arrange structure up to a point, but the audience will know and get irritated if I impose too much change. I also need to de-construct the well constructed grammar to colloquial dialogue, paring back constantly.

Giving the Books Theatrical Wings

And arching over all decisions is how can I make this theatrical? How can I bring my love and knowledge of theatre to tell the story all over again, not on the page but on the stage. That's the best bit, the most tantalising and most satisfying when the lights, the illusion, the music and the acting create something the book cannot. By inhabiting the story I can invent and expand, whilst always endeavouring to be true to the author's intentions. The majority of the audience for these shows are pre-teens, between eight and twelve, an age range that can be delightful and great fun. They have an emerging sense of humour and an excitement and enthusiasm for the world. To entertain them is a huge privilege and challenge.

Jacqueline Wilson's books are now sold all over the world, the proof of universal appeal. From my travels I've seen productions in many countries. A thousand and one experiences that all bear witness to the power of theatre and the recognition that children aren't so very different around the world. It's the societies they grow up in that set them apart and the power of a story, well told, that draws them together. My job is to give them theatrical wings. Life alongside Jacqueline Wilson has been a rich journey, full of adventures and experiences. Now the horizon is shifting and changing as I set off again with the next book, full of apprehension, of doubts but above all, enthusiasm. And I hope we continue to work and play together. The best tonic there is. For we don't stop playing because we grow old. We grow old because we stop playing.

Now to a List of the Ten T's for Children's Theatre Actors

1. **Talent:** Catch your clever actor and hold onto them. Persuade their agent that seven months touring to number one venues is a brilliant learning experience – rather than remaining out of work in the hope of catching one small TV job. It can often be difficult no matter how much the actor wants to work.

2. **Training:** Make sure the actor the basic skills of play and storytelling, the essence of our work. We are fiercely proud – so any whiff of a patronising attitude needs to be nipped in the bud. Most children's theatre is physically demanding so actors must be fit, have plenty of stamina, a real sense of humour, and be light on their feet in order to adjust.

3. **Time:** Fight for enough to dream, reflect, grow, harvest, refine, distil and polish.

4. **Teamwork:** Find talent and keep it together so a group grows respecting, admiring, liking and firing off each other. The result is a pleasure to watch, a group that has confidence, has ownership and exudes energy. And Tenacity. To carry on despite pettifogging pitfalls and problems.

5. **Thanks:** Encouragement for all involved which goes a long way towards nurturing aspiration.

6. **Try:** Try harder with each new production – not to be new, innovative, bigger or different. These are in words that are empty. Simply better. Better at making plays. Better at playing.

7. **Thick:** Only your skin that is – to withstand lack of recognition and reviews.

8. **Two:** Fingers to carry aloft even though misunderstood, maligned and patronised.

9. **Triumph:** That feeling when young people cheer at the curtain call and go out in animated conversation.

10. **Ten?** Ten green bottles of champagne to say 'well done.'

Vicky Ireland was Artistic Director of Polka Theatre, and is now freelance. She is involved in the promotion of children's theatre and literature through ACA (Association for Children's Arts).

STORY THEATRE AND FAMILY AUDIENCES

Toby Mitchell and Olivia Jacobs describe how a new company was formed for theatre which plays to children and adults in the same audience.

Tall Stories started by adapting Lewis Carroll's *Alice in Wonderland*, and Oscar Wilde's *The Happy Prince*. We presented them as high quality theatre at the Edinburgh Festival Fringe – and discovered our audience! Children and adults sharing the same theatre experience, responding to the imaginative worlds together.

An Alternative to Cinema-going

We seek to do in small-scale theatre what films like *Toy Story* and *Shrek* do for cinema audiences. Adults need to enjoy them as much as the kids (after all, they buy the tickets). Our productions all involve storytelling, with physical/visual theatre, music, songs and humour. We always start with a source story, whether a fairy tale, *Snow White*; a picture book, *The Gruffalo*; or a tale we have written ourselves, *Mum and the Monster*, in which a small boy searches for his missing mum.

The Company

It's very important to us that the performers are able to address the audience members directly, never patronising younger audience members, but rather challenging their imaginations. All of our work is devised, with the team of performers, director, designers, composers and the producer working together to create a script during rehearsals. We now have a pool of performers who have worked with us in the past (and we add to this pool every year), as well as some trusted designers lighting designers. Creating the script with the performers gives them a sense of ownership and involvement, and seems to bring a special quality to their performance.

Sometimes we have to train up stand-ins at a later date, and we always encourage them to bring their personality into the piece. Because of the nature of family-audience tour schedules (for the youngest audiences, mostly weekends and school holidays), we have now started involving more performers early in the devising process – then for the last two or three weeks of rehearsal, cutting down to the actual number needed for the first performances of the show. In this way, we have a pool of performers who are available for touring dates, all of whom have a sense of ownership of the piece, even if not actually in the first performances.

Theme and Narrative

It's important for us that our shows have strong themes, but we don't choose (or create) stories because of their themes – we choose them because of their strong narrative action.

Mum and the Monster: This was devised from a story written by us – a small boy's mum disappears, and his dad tells him she's been kidnapped by a monster. The boy sets off on a quest to find her, battling imaginary witches and giants on the way, only to find her with a new man. She had left it to her husband to explain the break up, not knowing that he would explain it through a story. The moment when the boy asks his mum 'Are you coming home?' and she replies 'No, not yet' is an example of the different ways children and adults interpret narrative events. We have found that for children, this seems to be just a part of a story, and not really related to their own life or that of someone they know. For adults, it is the worst thing in the world, as they imagine (or re-live) a family break up. For the whole audience, the moment is electric.

Snow White: There is possibly some subject matter that is truly taboo for family theatre, but we haven't found it yet. We went back to the original story, in which the Queen is Snow White's mother (not her stepmother), and in which the Queen eats what she thinks is Snow White's heart and liver. Although we state quite clearly these are actually the heart and liver of a deer that the Huntsman has killed in the forest, there were still sharp intakes of breath from the adults. Indeed, a theatre in America, who would otherwise have booked the show, told us, 'You can't do that in Texas.'

The Gruffalo: When we bought the theatrical rights to the picture book, we had no idea that the book was going to turn into a bestseller – we just knew it was a good story. We adapted it for a company of three storyteller-performers. Mouse is centre stage – she looks lost. A Narrator explains to us why she is there. She is beset by a series of predators (played by the same actor) who she outwits. Children accept stage conventions if the story is well told. We had not planned for the children to join in with the rhyming couplets, but when they did spontaneously, we incorporated this into the show. Some children will know the story – others not. At one point, we had put in an extra piece of action to give the performer playing the Gruffalo time to change into his costume. At this point in one performance, a small, frustrated-

PHOTO: TALL STORIES

The Gruffalo

looking boy, who knew the story by heart, stood up and declared loudly, 'This is where the Gruffalo comes on!'

Our Future as Storytellers

We have toured throughout England, Scotland, Wales and Ireland, performed in Warsaw's English Theatre, and toured extensively round Canada and the USA. Versions of our shows have been performed by companies in Australia, Singapore and Chile. From our productions we know there is a demand, not just for children's entertainment, but for quality theatre for the family audience.

We intend, and look forward to telling stories around the world in the future.

Toby Mitchell and Olivia Jacobs are co-directors of Tall Stories.

A PLAY FOR ACTORS AND YOUNG PERFORMERS

Claudette Bryanston describes a new form of theatre – actors and young people working together to interpret and perform a new play for an audience – young people's voices, young people's choices.

Founded in 1983 by Jenny Culank and myself, Classworks works with exceptional writers and playwrights, touring new plays. We have grown in artistic stature, experimenting with theatre form and new writing. Within this programme we have a commitment to theatre for young people. We have also developed a unique method to include young people's voices, and young people's choices in a professional production, working with experienced Actor-Facilitators and a Director. Young people take part in a Four day Residency – three days in the school and one day in the venue. The workshops include technical support enabling each group to produce their own music for the performance. We aim to develop both a high level educative process – and a high level of production/performance values. We have not been disappointed; in an atmosphere of professionalism young people give of their best.

In its recent touring work, the company is now ploughing back the seeds of discovery from these residency programmes, and the creative energy of its artists into our main touring productions, reaching a wide variety of venues and audiences. Much of the new writing is with established writers whose stories have captured the imagination of both young people and adults. Since 2000, Classworks has worked with Edward Bond, Mike Kenny, and now David Almond and Claire Macdonald with a new play *In Limbo*.

A New Form of Theatre

Bond wrote *The Children*, and a new form of theatre was born! This form of theatre combines adults and young people on stage, and places the young people centre stage to tell a powerful and compelling story. Bond sees the play as a 'rite of passage'. In *The Children* the young performers embark on a journey – a real journey from the start of the rehearsal process to the performance. The play itself is the story of a journey too; taking us through our social, intellectual and emotional world. It is a journey we all travel to try and understand the world.

'It's your play', Bond said to the seventeen young people who were the first cast. These were the young people who had inspired the playwright, a group of somewhat diffident, working-class pupils aged around fifteen, who live on a large council estate, and attend the same school. They were all perplexed – what did he mean? Bit by bit they realised the implications of Bond's words. *They* could tell the story using the words they wanted. *They* could make the decisions – where to be on stage, when to take the story, who to talk to, what to sign to the audience about the intensity of the dramatic situations they found themselves in. As we said in our publicity ' Adults have the text – and the young people must improvise.' How resonant are these words to young people trying to understand the world today?

Extract from Scene 5 The parts in this section played by young people

Joe sits alone. He is cold and hungry. Some of the Friends come on.

Friends: A kid's dead. That's serious.
They'll clobber us.
We didn't know he'd be dead.
Nor did Joe!
We didn't think. **That's** why he's dead.
We're all to blame.
We're not! **They're** to blame.
There wouldn't have been a fire if his mother hadn't said.

Silence. They look at each other. They stare at Joe. He sits with his head in his hands.

Joe: I can't manage it anymore. My hands – stink of petrol...
I wouldn't be alone.

Behind them a man (played by an actor) comes on slowly. He is tall and thin, his face is white, his hair is matted. He wears a long black overcoat, dark trousers, black boots and pearl-grey cloth gloves. He moves as if he does not see the others. He stops, stares at the ground. Falls.

The Friends turn to look at him. He lies completely still.

Sian, one of the young performers, said after the performance: 'This week really made me reflect on other people – and also how I act myself.' Can one ask more of an art form when such an experience enables us to empathise, and therefore to imagine and enrich the world? This experience of working with a playwright of world renown, who takes work for young people seriously, and the experience of working with adults and young people together, whetted our appetite for more. We were fascinated by the process of weaving the fixed writing for the adult actors with text that was free, and to be appropriated by the young performers.

The Second Collaboration

We asked Mike Kenny if he would write a play for us. Kenny is highly regarded by the young people's theatre community, and was delighted to write for such a large cast, not two or three actors as his usual commission, but maybe twenty performers. *Dictation* toured last autumn around the country. Kenny used the poetic cadence of Sophocles, but set his story of Antigone in a contemporary school.

Creon has become the Super-Head of a failing comprehensive school, Antigone, the pupil who challenges him, when her brother is left in the playground as an example to the rest. The pupils are constantly measured and tested. Finally a blind man who is wandering

Creon with Young Actors

159

around the school corridors enters his classroom, and shows him the truth. Creon at last sees his terrible error and resigns, but not before he has the blood of his star pupil on his hands.

Again the adult actor text was fixed. The young people had the freedom to improvise, and make their own choices – on stage. Again we had the unusual situation of adults and young people working together. As with *The Children* the actors as artists were clear about why the two projects were so extraordinary, and such a success. We learn together when we are working together. These plays will not work if we don't all journey together. The task is to tell a powerful story and over 1,600 young people performed these plays in professional venues and art centres across the country. Audiences were astonished at the quality of performance of the young people, the weight and strength of the productions themselves. Above all they came to the theatre and saw two very different and quite extraordinary plays.

Companies in Belgium, Holland and Australia are now working with *Dictation. The Children* is playing all over Europe and has been translated into several languages.

Future Productions

In 2005, we are touring with a beautiful version of a short story by leading children's writer David Almond from his autobiographical book *Counting Stars*. Our adaptation is called *In Limbo* and is a real *coup de théâtre*. In co-production with the Belgrade Theatre, Coventry, we also plan an adaptation of Derrek Hines epic poem – a visual spectacular set in modern day Iraq of the epic *Gilgamesh*; literally Poetry in Motion.

In our twenty-first year we are in the privileged position of combining experience and expertise with a growing team of established writers and designers. We are fortunate to work with young people as actors, who will be the next generation of theatre audience. We are able to experiment with a glorious art form, in which we can see the immediate impact of our work, and know also that for many, their early experience of theatre will be something they will remember all their lives.

Claudette Bryanston is Co-Artistic Director of Classworks.

6. THEATRE-IN-EDUCATION AND THEATRE IN SCHOOLS

A PRIMARY THEATRE-IN-EDUCATION PROGRAMME

Ian Yeoman takes us through the aims, process and outcomes of a learning session. The session alternates between theatre images and action – and sections where the children use their imaginations.

Pre-performance: It's the start of the school day. A class of children are in the school hall, sitting in a semi-circle, looking at a life-sized square frame. Inside, an actor sits on a throne in a life-sized portrait frame. He wears a robe, a crown, and a leather glove for his hunting hawk. At his feet, a loaf of bread. He is the central character in the story being acted out – *The King*.

> *An Actor-Teacher invites the children to project themselves imaginatively into the King's viewpoint: … as the King looks out across his land, what can he see, smell, touch and taste of his Kingdom?*

The children suggest: … a bridge across the river between his castle and the town … people on the bridge … farmers going to the market … servants on their day off from working in the King's kitchens

Actor-Teacher: What could be the name of this bridge?

One of the class: Castle Bridge.

The play begins: The King took to his bed seven years ago. His people feel that he is failing in his responsibility as King. He is disgusted by his own image. He decrees that every mirror in the Kingdom be broken. By a mound of stones, a Young Girl grieves for her Mother, who has died after the breaking of the mirrors. The Young Girl listens to a Music Box – *I can hear my Mother's voice!* She looks into a mirror – *I can see my Mother's face!*

> *The children participate. The class gather round the stones. A child lifts the stones. They find a Hair Ribbon – the Music Box – and a Hand Mirror.*

Actor-Teacher: Who does the mirror belong to?

Children: ... a gift from the Mother to the Child ... the last mirror in the kingdom.

The Actor-Teacher sets up an image of the Young Girl sitting by the stones and invites the class to place the objects in the picture. They decide to use the Hair Ribbon to connect the Young Girl's hand, the Music Box and the Mirror.

PHOTO: KEITH MORRIS

Lifting the stones

Actor-Teacher: The ribbon is like a bridge ... What could this bridge be called?

One child: ... the ribbon bridge of memory.

Actor-Teacher responds: The 'ribbon bridge of memory'. Is it as strong as the Castle Bridge?

Children's responses: No! ... if the King discovers she has a mirror ... he'll destroy the bridge!

The children in role: The class are now the town's people at a public meeting. They talk about the problem of the King's ban on mirrors. They use the objects from the story experience to show the King how his people are feeling.

A bridge (made out of piles of books) ... between ignorance and learning ... it's weak and in need of repair ... everyone needs a bridge ... from now to the past ... if bridges are destroyed we've no idea where we're going ... the old people remember where the bridges are ... mirrors are important ... we can see where we've come from ... we can remember what's important!

'Imaginative' insights become a tool for 'conceptual' learning. In this session the Actor-Teachers drew on an observation the children made – a bridge separating the King and his castle from the life activity of his people – then later applied this idea of the bridge at a metaphorical level. The children related the idea of the ribbon bridge to the young girl – her situation and individual psychology. The idea of a physical bridge, and bridging feelings developed in stages as a tool to deepen their conceptual understanding.

In the story of the young girl, we see her struggling to make sense of her own life and relationships. We also see the King, and the social forces of his kingdom. Drama conventions facilitate the exploration of an individual life situation and the objective conditions, so insight and understanding can begin.

The Drama World and the Real World: Having rendered the complexity of the world and our place in it tangible and available for exploration, the TIE programme then requires that children and young people to define it and take action. In requiring the active intervention of the participants, the programme demands that new knowledge, ideas and intuitions are tested in practice. The action required in TIE is social action; the children work together. They work collectively and are aware that their actions have implications attached to them. They take action consciously and transform the fictional world they are exploring. 'They listen, communicate, challenge and support one another.' They know that they may not have resolved everything, but they feel that they have achieved some development.

Theatr Powys has developed key concerns: Story and Ideology, Cultural Identity, the Natural Environment, Learning and Teaching, What History is, Social Responsibility. These cultural concerns underpin many of the curriculum areas that teachers are engaging children with on a day-to-day basis in the school. However, we do not want to develop work that will simply assist in the delivery of fixed categories of knowledge related to curriculum areas defined in Key Stages. We do not wish to be an illustrated lesson attached to an attainment target. Rather, the work can support teachers in engaging the critical imagination of their students in exploring fundamental questions affecting all areas of human experience. The child's experience of our work can illuminate (and is transferable) to all other aspects of their educational experience. We work with a high actor/teacher-child ratio. We are trying to create work that meets the needs of children and young people as developing human beings, who exist within the context of their schools, their families, their wider communities and the world in its totality. Responses to the work suggest that we are right to maintain this approach.

Principles of Theatre-in-Education Method

- insists on the centrality of imagination and creativity – the images of theatre endure in the mind when facts are long forgotten
- treats education as a process, where children exercise power as active seekers after truth
- acts on the recognition that children have experiences and concerns that go to the heart of being human
- is a unity of culture – young people striving for a better world

Ian Yeoman is Director of Theatre Powys.

PARTICIPATORY THEATRE IN ACTION

Anthony Haddon gives an overall picture of Theatre Blah Blah Blah's ideals and aims, and takes the reader into the specific skills of leading a participatory workshop for pupils.

A Learning Organisation

Our aim is to follow the Blah no matter how hopeless and no matter how far, inspired by the lyrics of the song: *The Impossible Dream*. Our policy is to make theatre wherever we are, and do it because we want to do it.

- We make theatre based on stories and ideas that interest us, then find ways to engage you the audience
- We work on ideas and stories over a two/three year period experimenting with different formats with different audiences, taking time to find the best way to tell a story, and the reason we are telling it
- Our approach is like a trip into the unknown, so we see the Blahs as a 'learning organisation' involving the audience in the process with us

Set up in 1985, the youth service adopted the company, and we began creating theatre work for young people, touring youth centres then secondary schools in Leeds as well as village halls on rural touring circuits and residencies in theatres. There is a core company of three people and a Board of Directors made up of academics, theatre practitioners, business people, teachers, freelance actors, designers, writers, musicians and educationalists. We receive core funding from the Arts Council of England; Leeds City Council contributes to running costs, with free office and rehearsal space. In 1991, we began working through the educational workshops which led us into Participatory Theatre.

Participatory Workshop Theatre – *Barkin'* by Mark Catley (based on Melvin Burgess novel *Lady – My Life as a Bitch*).

Meet Mitzy the dog – former housewife and mother. One of the strange encounters that Sandra has when, aged seventeen, she herself is accidentally turned into a dog – just at the point in her life when she is enjoying the power of her sexuality. We follow her into the dog world, and her attempts to get her family to accept her as – a bitch. Her mother can see the real Sandra behind that growling and big sloppy tongue, but no one else will accept her, even though they have to admit that this dog knows a lot about their missing girl. After trying to fit in Sandra decides being a dog doesn't feel so bad after all – look at Mitzy.

The audience (60) watch the one hour play in the round. Then are invited to step into this strange world by accepting that if true – how would a documentary team investigate the story? Who would they need to interview? Actor-Facilitators work with them in groups, with video cameras and set up interviews with key participants. They then view their resulting documentary – or 'dog-u-mentary'. We need surrealism in education!

Participatory Primary School Programme

Primary schools approached the Blahs to create a stimulus that would engage their pupils with reading and writing in Years 5 and 6 (nine and ten year-olds). We chose to explore George Eliot's novel *Silas Marner*.

Silas Marner: We have a team of four Actor-Teachers working with one group of thirty pupils for a two hour session. We will work with them for three more two hour sessions over the next four weeks. One actor enters the performance space wearing a rough-looking jacket, which has a timeless quality to it, and carrying a sack over his back. The actor walks around the edge of the space, mostly head down, but sometimes looking around.

> **Facilitator:** I want you to take a close look at this man. (*There is a long pause as we all look.*) Tell me what you see.
> **Pupil:** He looks lost.
> **Facilitator:** Yes he does, what is it about him that looks lost? (*throws the question out to everybody*)
> **Pupil:** He doesn't seem to know where he is.
> **Facilitator:** How is he showing that?
> **Pupil:** You can tell by his eyes.

Facilitator: Can you show me what he was doing with his eyes? (*Pupil scrunches her eyes up in the manner of the actor*)
Facilitator: How does that make you feel?
Pupil: Like everything is strange.

The actor is doing the most simple of actions, walking around the space as if undertaking a long journey, and looking for something. The action is informed by the entire history of that character's history to date, but the pupils don't know anything about that history. They have never heard of Silas Marner, or the novelist George Eliot – or that George Eliot was in fact a woman who wrote this novel in 1860, and set it in England in the 1820's just at the end of the Napoleonic Wars. This is the beginning of a drip-feed of information, a skill that every experienced playwright and storyteller has learned to master.

So we have begun with action, and that is the level we keep our first conversation at, because we want to play to the pupils' strengths as sign-readers. I am talking about visual sign in the way Dorothy Heathcote uses it in Drama-in-Education – the verbal sign as much as the written sign. The pupils begin to realise we are asking them to offer their observations, and that there doesn't seem to be a right or a wrong answer. They are beginning to trust us, and realising this space we are sitting around may be a space for play.

A Journey into a Novel

It is important that we gain the trust of these pupils, because a lot of them are under-achieving in writing and reading, and we are all about to embark on a journey into a novel usually set for high level study. The National Curriculum in Literacy Key Stage 2 gave us the freedom to choose any classic text and Barnaby King, Associate Director, chose this story because it has a child at the centre. The Oxford Reading Tree publish an abridged child-friendly version of *Silas Marner*, which helps build up our trust with teachers. The teachers were not to introduce the text to the children until we had begun the programme.

Facilitator: I am going to tell you something about this man. He has left his home forever. He is looking for somewhere new to live.

This rounds off our first conversation about the man we are looking at, and confirms their observations, but places a new question. Why would he have left his home forever? We do not ask them directly, but instead get them to answer it through a less direct approach.

Facilitator: He is carrying the weight of the world on his shoulders – *(pause, with a mystified tone)* – what does that mean?'

The pupils split into smaller groups and tackle the phrase.
Pupil: Maybe he has left his family behind, and that troubles him.
Pupil: Or his house has burnt down, and he can never return to it.
Pupil: It's his head that weighs like the world.
Facilitator: Why?
Pupil: He's anxious. He doesn't know where he is going to live.

Facilitator reports to the whole group. So this man is weighed down by the weight of all his possessions in his sack, and anxieties about the future which are turning over in his mind making his head very heavy on his shoulders. He can hardly keep his head up as he walks along.

The whole group are beginning to own this man with a sack on his back. They are beginning to get pulled into his story. The deeper they dig, the more there is to understand about this man. We indicate to the children that there are things in this drama we cannot make sense of, without them being there to witness the events with us, and contribute their ideas. We are drawing them in, using questioning skills.

Open and Closed Questions

The Blahs have spent eleven years working with Drama-in-Education specialist, Eileen Pennington, in practical applications of Dorothy Heathcote's approach to teaching through drama. Eileen made us aware of the importance of asking 'open' questions, and 'closed' questions.

We began the whole programme asking the children to tell us what they saw. They could say anything. That requires the Actor-Teacher to improvise, and take on any comment and find its place in our drama. If a question is put across as an open invitation to contribute, but really the Actor-Teacher is looking for a particular answer, then the children will sense there is a right answer to guess and you will send mixed messages to the children. At the beginning of the drama, we had planted signs for them to read, the costume, the gestures of the actor, but we could never guarantee where their observations would begin, or how confident they would be to share what they saw.

This approach to working with children requires the actor to learn teaching skills, and be ready to invest more time in facilitating children's contributions than performing to them. The programme also had sections where the actors performed scenes in front of the children, spread equally throughout the sessions.

Facilitator: *(We are all watching the actor walk around the space)* What do you think he has got in his sack?
Pupil: Pots and pans.
Facilitator: Yes, he may not know where his next meal is coming from. He may have to stop and cook something himself.
Pupil: He might not have enough money to buy any food.
Facilitator: What kind of food would last a long journey?
Pupil: Cheese, fruit and biscuits.
Facilitator: So just after he has eaten a piece of cheese, and he is ready to settle down for the night he gets something out of his sack, something that reminds him of where he came from, something that he looks at every night ... *(the actor acts out the scene as the suggestions come in).*
Pupil: A letter.
Facilitator: It is in an envelope *(the actor mimes unfolding the envelope).*
Pupil: He has folded it up really tightly.
Pupil: He doesn't want to look inside.
Facilitator: Has he read the letter inside?
Pupil: Yes, he reads it every night.

We get three or four suggestions for creatures from the children and then wrap their observations into the next piece of narrative.

Facilitator: When this man arrived at the place where he made his new home, the local people saw him in the distance just a silhouette against the sky and one of them said that there is a snail. Of course he was just a man. I can now tell you his name is Silas Marner, and this story took place in England one hundred and eighty years ago. We are now going to the place where he came from.

Continuation of the Programme

What I have described here is the first thirty minutes of an eight hour session in which we use a number of drama conventions to keep the children engaged with the story. Sometimes the pupils are in role as children from the village where Silas makes his new home, or they are witnesses to people's private lives. At one point in the drama, we have the entire class sitting behind the dressing table in the Squire's bedroom while we overhear conversations between the Squire and his wife about their inability to have children – snippets of conversation that span fifteen years.

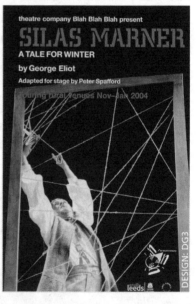

theatre company Blah Blah Blah present

SILAS MARNER

A TALE FOR WINTER

by George Eliot

Adapted for stage by Peter Spafford

touring rural venues Nov–Jan 2004

leeds

DESIGN: DG3

They have the opportunity to talk directly to the characters, such as Godfrey who reveals to them that he married a woman he did not love because he had got her pregnant. The child from that marriage will be adopted by Silas Marner, and she will grow up loving Silas as a father not knowing who her true parents were. Silas names the child Eppie. In the final session, Godfrey decides that he is going to tell the truth and reveal to Eppie, who is now seventeen, that he is her father, and that he can offer her a comfortable life as the daughter of a Squire.

We do not see that scene played out. We ask the pupils to speak for Eppie, and decide what she would say to Godfrey.

Pupil: I will come as long as Silas can come with me, as he looked after me. Because he's poor and he's old, and he can't look after himself

Pupil: I won't come. Silas has taken your place now.

How and why we extended our contact time in schools

The first six years of touring work to schools and youth centres, was very creative. Contact-time was an hour-long show, and an hour workshop. Youth centres are only open for two hours a night, and schools do not usually release their students for more than two hours in a day. Also we have to charge a fee, and not many places could afford to bring us in for more than one visit per year.

I had two impulses to break out of this format. The first, the more I experimented with putting children in role, the more time was needed to develop their work. Secondly, I wanted to see the impact our work could have on children's learning. The Blahs began to create eight-hour workshop programmes. It is a challenge to find funding for this work. Artistically it is labour-intensive. We have found support from 'Creative Arts Projects In Education' which funds professional creative people to work alongside teachers. We were also funded by an Educational Action Zone with a commitment to creativity in its six primary schools.

Actor and Collaborator

Actors who respond to this way of working are able to see how they can extend their dramatic skills beyond the formal relationship of actor and spectator – into actor and collaborator. When you are working at this level of participation it begs the question of whether it is easier to train a teacher to act, or an actor to teach. In my experience actors bring conviction in the truth of the fictional world we are working in, and teachers discover the power of engaging children just by playing a character. The best team is a mixture of actors and teachers.

Participatory drama is a true meeting point between the worlds of education and the arts, worlds which should never have been separated in the first place.

Anthony Haddon is Director of Theatre Blah Blah Blah.

CHILDREN'S THEATRE AND EMOTIONAL LITERACY –
The Air Raid Warning sounds!

Jain Boon on how Gwent Theatre devised a play conveying the experience of evacuee children for schools audiences – developing the ability to respond to and articulate emotional experience.

Home Front was devised by Gwent Theatre, and written by Philip Michell. It has three performers (Duncan Alexander, Jain Boon, Jessica Torr) is set during the Second World War, and is targeted at Top Junior/Lower Secondary school pupils.

The Devising Process

Historical Research. The project began with Philip researching three main topics: women at work, the Blitz, the evacuation of children from cities and industrial areas. Particularly important and poignant were the personal recollections, some of which contained harrowing stories of abuse. Early on in the devising process we developed the idea of three children on a bombsite who, through their play and interaction, revealed their highly personal and individual experiences as evacuees.

Character Improvisation: Along with the writer, the company explored material through improvisation, some based on true experiences, and characters were developed from different home and social backgrounds. Each actor chose one particular character. The writer and designer filled the rehearsal room with pieces of costume, fabric, props and an assortment of junk related to the period. Philip then asked the actors to build an environment from the materials provided, and they were given a brief. This produced the most absorbing improvisation he had ever witnessed. The exercise lasted an hour, and the three central characters emerged: a girl lost on her way home, a running boy, and a girl with her drawing book. They became the base to tell the story. These characters were deepened through 'hot-seating' – a technique where each actor in turn sits on a central chair, as the character they are developing. The other actors ask personal questions to which the actor in role improvises responses – this establishes the circumstances and inner life of each character.

Scenario: This was constructed from ideas generated by looking at photographs of the period, prompting us to experiment with the creation of three images/still tableaux. It was decided that these would be placed at the opening of the play offering the audience a snapshot of each of these children's stories.

Set and Design: (Bettina Reeves) An abstract space, could be a bombsite, could be a nowhere place. We discussed the idea that these children were in some sort of limbo, tied to a place they could not leave, for they had to keep telling their stories over and over again. The design came out of the workshop described above. It consisted of a floor cloth surrounded by objects of the period and what appeared to be a door standing on its own, children's clothes hanging on a washing line and two step-ladders.

Music: (Chrys Blanchard) The music was written specifically for the play and allowed us to have a feel of the period whilst serving the particular needs of the characters and stories. Themes were repeated in different styles depending on the mood. 'Dona Nobis Pacem' a song sung in church-style allowed for reflection, whilst at another moment it is changed, and used to resemble the motion of a train. Some songs are given the 'stiff upper lip' treatment, the melancholic lyrics coupled with the joyful tune.

The Play in Performance

Three children enter the space. First, a girl (Joyce) who sits and draws in a book. Followed by another girl (Elizabeth) who concentrates on packing and unpacking her case, paying particular attention to three objects in it. She moves to another space and repeats her routine. A boy (Ifor) enters/trots rhythmically around the perimeter of the stage. None of the children acknowledge each other's presence. They are on their own. A wailing air raid siren is heard. The children huddle together with their backs to each other as if in a small shelter. Music – 'Dona Nobis Pacem – during this the children form images, one from each of their stories.

– Joyce and her mum, waving goodbye to Dad carrying a kit bag
– A woman farmer examining Ifor's teeth as if he were an animal, while a dog (an actor wearing a gas mask) sits close to his side
– A woman and man comforting Elizabeth

Each image is created in an area onstage, and held for a few seconds before the actors break to form the next image placed in another area. The sequence is repeated three times. We return to the siren, then the 'all clear' is heard. The children return to their huddle and then to their initial activities. After a short while, Elizabeth finishes packing her case, looks lost and bursts into tears – this is the start of the relationship that develops. Joyce is a child who wants to help and is very caring ensuring that no one is ever left out. Elizabeth appears to be selfish and insensitive; she finds it hard to play or use her imagination and is a bully. Ifor does not speak, but through the period of the play he engages more and more.

We discover the children are all on their way home towards the end of the war. As they play, memories are sparked which reveal to our audience the person-al experiences of their lives prior to, and during their time of evacuation. We return to their present lives to discover what effect it has had on them. The stories were carefully woven, not only to give the audience a sense of back-ground to the war but to show how each of these children survived

An emotional parting

their own emotional baggage through the care, or lack of care of their 'foster' parents.

Theatre Experience and Emotional Literacy

In effect, we have examined why these characters are who they are, why they behave in the way they do and what is important to them. We are asking our young people to look at the whole person, and not to judge too quickly. Through exploring the lives of these three children, our young audience are developing a vocabulary for thoughts and feelings. In the after-show discussion with our audience, I am always surprised at how able these young children are at articulating and recognising the characters' thoughts and feelings. They are able to pick up on what is unsaid, more so than with some of our older audiences.

Teachers have spoken to us about 'the child who has barely spoken in two years', yet was able to articulate a particular character's wants and needs. Always satisfying of course is 'the child' who gives way to feelings, allowing themselves to let go and show emotion – the one who may usually be giving the teachers 'attitude.' A child who was fascinated by the character Elizabeth recognised something in her that was similar to himself – he had Asperger's Syndrome. Teachers at the performance and after-show discussion may be surprised by a particular child's reaction.

Home Front has now had three tours (notice how important that number has been). The 2004 tour was used as a Transition Project for pupils leaving Primary School and entering Secondary School. Continued support and guidance for pupils was available throughout the summer break following through into the new academic year. Its success is marked by the amount of times we are asked to tour the play, how well it is received by our audiences and teachers and from their responses on evaluation forms. As practitioners, we are highly critical of our work – always searching to do better.

Young people's emotional literacy is not tied to their academic literacy. Theatre provides an effective context for its development and expression.

Jain Boon directs for the Gwent Theatre company.

INVESTIGATIVE THEATRE IN SECONDARY SCHOOLS

Roundabout Company at Nottingham Playhouse. Andrew Breakwell takes us through the principles of 'investigative theatre'. He describes the stages in co-developing a social education play dealing with asylum seekers with the Thalia Theatre, Hamburg.

Roundabout was set up in 1973 as the Theatre-in-Education Company at Nottingham Playhouse. Its remit was to tour schools with plays and interactive programmes, enhancing the work of teachers across the curriculum. The introduction of the National Curriculum by the Thatcher government made it necessary to change company practice. Participatory, open-ended TIE programmes were replaced. Roundabout continued to tour schools, challenging students and teachers and raising important issues of the time, but now through well-crafted, energetically performed plays.

In recent years some of our plays have been seen in Europe *Warrior Square* by Nick Wood and *Stepping on the Cracks* by Mike Kenny were performed at the Frankfurt ASSITEJ Conference in 2001. In 2002, *The Night Maze* was performed at the European Theatre Convention Festival in Bratislava. Recently the company was invited to Nova Gorica in Slovenia with our production of *Mohammed*, as part of the European Community accession celebrations. Again this was organized through the ETC – the European Theatre networking organization which has brought immense benefits. For a wide range of audiences, the company's concern has been theatre that has resonance and meanings for our home constituency, but is influenced by, and made with, companies and individuals from abroad.

Theatre and the World of – What if?

What are the pedagogic principles that underpin these plays? Essentially, the act of watching theatre and indeed making it, requires a dialogue to make the meanings of the play relevant to an audience. Each person in the group will bring their own perceptions of the world. So the drama must aim to raise questions in the minds of the viewer about the ideas explored, and the worlds revealed through the play. This is an essential element of democratic debate and leads to a political view of the world. The play itself, the post-show discussion, the drama workshop, the experience arising from the drama all challenge perceptions of the known world and take the audience to the world of – what if? In that speculation and debate we exercise the essential faculties that are required by a functioning and participative democracy. These are the principles of education that underpin the range of plays we try to develop and deliver.

Is there a better way than collaborative working?

Investigating the lives of Asylum Seekers

Roundabout was commissioned last year to develop and deliver an interactive package to schools on race awareness. I turned to a European model – *Mohammed* by Neilsen and Seligman. This is a Danish 'classroom play' predicated upon the dynamic dramatic tension of the 'audience' (i.e. the students) believing the characters might be real, and that their plight requires a genuine response. I took the play, broke it into segments, added question and answer sessions, a visual Powerpoint projection of responses and information, and played it in an informal setting to a small audience.

We meet two Iranian asylum seekers, Reza and his wife Maryam. We find out why the family are now asylum seekers. Through 'investigative theatre' the pupils question them, find out about their situation, come to understanding them, and challenge preconceptions.

Reza and Maryam

Hot-seating: Then to explore and understand the real life involved, a pupil puts on Maryam's scarf, takes on the role of an asylum seeker mother, and responds to questions from the other pupils.

The participating pupils were ten and eleven year olds, in what in the days of the mining industry were called 'coalfield villages'. Today there are no mines and few new jobs – the pupils themselves are in an area of economic deprivation. We were able to raise questions – what is an economic migrant, an asylum seeker, a refugee? This is 'investigative theatre' as developed in the 80's. It is very effective in changing attitudes through analysis and debate. Pupils also talked with and questioned real outsiders about their life experiences.

A pupil in role of Maryam

Actor and Audience – Revisiting TIE

Something interesting was happening, processes were being redefined and challenges laid down. In essence, how could I now utilize years of experience of making plays for a variety of stages, and respond to the most essential theatrical convention – actor and an audience? What is there in the working methods of TIE, that we might now relevantly re-visit with profit?

Nick Wood, the dramatist (recent winner of the Brothers Grimm award in Germany) put it as follows: 'An actor facing a group of students in a classroom. No area marked out as the performance space.

No distance between the performer and the audience. A challenge for both of them. In particular many more choices than in a conventionally staged piece. Each room will be different. Each member of the audience will face the actor as an individual, not as a member of a group. No one will have anywhere to hide. It's important that both actor and audience don't feel threatened or unsafe. It's not a confrontation between them, but a journey they go on together.'

We are now working together with Corinna Honold and Andrea Udl from Thalia Theatre, Hamburg, to make a new play for classrooms – *Mia* – to be performed in both Nottingham and Hamburg. The play will be jointly developed in a series of discussions and workshop sessions, and the directors at both theatres will swap approaches and rehearsal techniques. So what will *Mia* be about and what form will it take?

We use the same classroom technique. This time it is Mia who is visiting the school. She is looking for her fourteen year old sister. She has lost her home, and some of her family. Her search has given her a sense of purpose; even though she doubts she will be successful she has to continue. She is difficult, feisty, awkward, very bright, full of nervous energy. The girls like her, the boys find her attractive, but, truth to tell, she's a little bit too scary for them.

Theatre as Investigative Laboratory

The dramatic device to involve the pupils this time is to investigate something physical. Mia has a collection of assorted bits and pieces in her bag. She shows them to the class. All of the objects, except one, are things she has found. She doesn't make up stories about the things – she waits to see what story they will tell her. She is always in the stories, of course, that's the whole point. There is a comb with broken teeth, that she didn't find, it belonged to her sister. Gradually, as she feels she has gained their trust, she lets out little bits of her past. She reveals she is of Roma background but she is very careful who she tells. She has come to ask the school if she may speak to the pupils about her lost sister. Have they seen her, do they know anything about her? She tells the class about her sister. Shows them a photograph. Tells them about the comb. Confesses her fears about what has happened to her, and why she was abducted. She puts her bits and pieces back into her bag, and as she does so, she picks up a stone. She hasn't been able to find a story for this one yet. She looks around and gives it to one of the boys. He accepts it and starts to be the person who can unlock its story…

We have met a young woman having to face being uprooted from her home, and the loss of her sister. Despite what has happened to

Mia shows a photograph

her, she won't let it beat her. She still has her sense of the ridiculous, her anger, her pride, and her compassion. The class should want to help her, know they can't help, and probably doubt if she will be successful in her search. But what is important is that they see she won't be beaten. And that they learn about the circumstances in which her life has fallen apart. They will have to confront their own prejudices when they find out who she is, and they have empathised with her as a person, rather than as a member of a despised group.

Perhaps most importantly for the young people's audience, there is also no place for them to hide, and there lies the challenge for the writer, director and actor.

Mia: What would it take to make you leave your country? I don't say for a holiday, for one or two years, but probably forever? Can you think of anything bad enough that might happen to you here to make you want to do that? Then you are very lucky people.

After the Play

The production in each school will be followed by pupil interaction with real asylum seekers and refugees, resident in Nottingham. They will talk with them, ask questions, share their feelings and hopefully at the end of the exercise, understand just a little better what it means to have had to leave a home, travel to a different country and make a new life in strange surroundings with a language they don't comprehend. This political understanding is one of the major challenges for our society and it is hardly surprising that our play is just one of many from all over Europe that examines the themes of dislocation, movement and refuge.

Worlds will have been changed, meanings made, perceptions altered and horizons lifted through the drama and the answering of all those – what if – questions that our Theatre Laboratory provides. Developing this piece of theatre, and the accompanying activities with our European colleagues, makes Roundabout a vital and significant part of our educational and artistic communities here in Nottingham.

Andrew Breakwell is Director of Roundabout and Education at Nottingham Playhouse. He has worked in educational theatre since 1970, and at the Playhouse since 1999. He directs plays for both the main stage and schools tours. He is committed to developing cross-European links.

7. THEATRE FOR SPECIAL AUDIENCES

EARLY YEARS THEATRE

Carey English recounts her research and developmental projects and how it has informed Quicksilver's development of effective theatre for Early Years audiences.

In the 1980's Quicksilver Theatre produced several shows for children aged three to seven years. Whilst performing in them, I had a growing need to investigate, just who were behind those rows of faces – willing, but sometimes blank – belonging to the youngest members of the audience. The older children would engage with the performance enthusiastically and noisily, which could at times unsettle the little ones. It was clear to me that three to five year olds needed some theatre especially for them. Thankfully, I was not alone in my thinking. With an Arts Council Bursary I began what has become an on-going process of observation of small people.

Children's Play – a Rehearsal for Life

Sixteen years later, much of what I have learnt seems so obvious. Little children of this age are society at large writ small; they are competent, fully-established personalities who live in the moment; their emotions are overwhelming – great monsters that will eat them at night, or catch them just around a corner. Children's play is their rehearsal for life. There is huge range in their play. Domestic – playing house, making food, looking after 'babies', mummies and daddies. Archetypal fantasy – fairies, kings, queens. Experiments with power through superhero, magic and gun play. Action replay of events that have made an impact on them – hospitals, doctors, stand up lovers' rows. Endless dinosaur play. Physical play – exploring how things are, e.g. in large construction, just how tall a tower can you build before it all falls over?
   Through play, children develop their understanding of the world. Play is where they construct their identity by externalising their emotions and experiences, fantasy and real. In play, they re-create and repeat those bits of life they need to 'run past themselves again'

– so that they can learn for themselves how they feel about something, experiment with how they would react given the same situation again, and affirm for themselves their response to a situation. How similar to the actor working on a character in rehearsal! In play they confront everything from danger and deep sadness, to complete joy and the boldly mundane; they address the archetypes of good and evil, the greatness of loss, the novelty of power, the heights of love, anger, the curiosity of how things are so, with passion, commitment and tenacity, with everything, in fact, that you could hope to see on a stage. In one word, drama. I was completely humbled. How could any adult presume to know what theatre such ably dramatic beings would enjoy? Dare we presume to establish drama workshops for them, when they patently create drama for themselves all the time?

Dramatic Story-Building Workshop

I developed a Drama Workshop with writer Cheryl Moskowitz, where a class-sized group of children could share emotions, and build a storyline together with a shared sense of achievement. We called this 'Dramatic Story Building'. The process offers signposts to shape the building blocks of setting, character, conflict and resolution. We were able to accept every child's idea by using 'comparative and superlative' to establish an agreed idea. Children at this age have a fascination with 'good, better, best'; 'some, more, the most'. To establish character and setting we began by asking them to think of something big, something bigger and then the biggest thing they could think of. To introduce conflict, 'scary, scarier, scariest thing'. To introduce resolution, 'something strong, stronger, strongest'. Asking open questions to get more detail embellished each idea. Finally to finish on a positive ending, we would ask them what the happiest thing was, because we had discovered that little children actually want everything to be all right in the end – they need to feel safe. They could even go as far as compassion; they often want to make friends with the demons they have vanquished.

There was precious little theatre for three to fives in the late 80's. We were eager to pass this method on, and to share with other theatre practitioners the news that three to five years-olds are a fascinating and challenging audience who teach us all a thing or two about life, and theatre. We also needed to know more about child development. With Arts Council support, Jo Belloli and I organised the first ever conference on Theatre for Under-5's in the UK. In fact, it addressed the three to five year-old age group. Theatre for Under-3's only began to develop later with Theatre-rites' play, *Lost and Moated Land*, in 1977. Theatre practitioners, children's authors, nursery teachers and early years specialists gathered for a weekend about child development, improvising form and content, learning through skills workshops, and confronting the issues of theatre for three to fives. This was a pivotal event which galvanised many companies and individuals to go on to develop some astounding work for the age group including Mike Kenny, Amanda and Tim Webb of Oily Cart Theatre, Paul Harman of CTC, and Penny Bernand who established Theatre-rites.

What sort of Theatre should we be making for the 3 to 5's?

The Child Development specialists told us three to fives want from theatre everything that adults want for themselves, from musicals to the catharsis of emotions – with provisos: death is taboo, as is genital sexuality. Drama should therefore draw its deepest themes from the powerful feelings children have at this stage. It's a rich age when character is formed and morality and conscience is developed. 'Make good triumph over evil. Emotionally, any theme is possible (except the irreversibility of death) and they will love it all.' I agree that any theme is possible, but I also believe that it is important to address the theme of death, provided it is done with great sensitivity. The advice was to be rigorously honest; be aware that their boundaries between fiction and reality are tenuous, and they are therefore vulnerable; and always challenge your assumptions of what constitutes a child's world.

We asked ourselves lots of questions about the function of theatre. Should we engage with the age-old battle of good v. evil, or focus more on replicating real-life experiences? Should we address pressure points specifically – a new sibling, the approach of big school, family quarrels? How can we use fear without real danger? Should we use archetype or stereotype? Are we in danger of imposing an adult morality?

What forms can theatre for three to fives take? Is participation a vital element or should drama allow a child a private involvement? Do children accept adults playing children, and animals? How can music, puppetry and other skills be absorbed? How many actors and points of focus? We also had questions about the setting. Where should a child encounter theatre – in a safe and familiar base or in a special, exciting place? How should the experience be prepared for and followed up?

Quicksilver Theatre's Plays

The plays for that followed from Quicksilver in the early 90's were commissioned from freelance writers. *Granny's Bottom Drawer* by Cheryl Moskowitz about being old and being young.

Pretend We're Friends by Robin Kingsland about how friendship is negotiated between strangers.

The Sound Collector by Roger McGough, about friendship, betrayal and sound.

Whose Shoes? by Mike Kenny, about sibling rivalry. These plays answered some of the questions. They encompassed a range of themes, were a mix of storytelling, some with songs or poems, some reflected real life, others were complete fantasy, and bold in their use of archetype.

It was clear that a specific three to five years audience was needed. The youngest children were no longer intimidated by enthusiastically noisy seven year-olds, and the pace was gentler. Performances became more intimate when we decided to limit the audience size to eighty. Small children are more comfortable in smaller audiences. They feel more involved, that the show is especially for them.

The Journey as a Writer and Director

I now felt confident to attempt writing and directing with Guy Holland, co-artistic director at Quicksilver Theatre.

One reason children will watch drama is because they can identify with a character's struggle and be relieved that someone else is taking the strain for a change. They might also watch it because it's fun, and makes them laugh and smile. Humour is really important in theatre for three to fives. Statistics tell us that little children smile and laugh over four hundred times a day, and the average adult manages something short of thirty times. Humour engages and reassures.

Magic Mirrors: This first play was based on the familiar early years theme of Me – Myself. It began with the smell of frying onions cooking off-stage. It was about those odd moments when you are four years-old, your mum has told you that lunch is nearly ready, it takes forever and you fill the moment in the living room with playing with something there – a mirror. Our heroine's reflection comes alive, entices her into the mirror, and she is off on a journey of self-discovery, meeting challenges and overcoming them, making several friends, and learning how to blow her nose, returning just in time for lunch. Much of it quite surreal and whimsical, with plenty of familiar experiences and challenges for them to recognise. None of it really scary.

Friendly Feelings: The following play showed how being friends is a source of power in childhood. Can I be your friend? You're my friend aren't you? I won't be your friend if… Staying overnight in another family's home is a big deal, because not only is everything different, and your mum isn't there, but your friend calls all the shots because it's their place. Life can often be like playing a game, but you don't know what the rules are. This was another play about negotiating friendship – relationships can be the slipperiest things as an adult. As a child they can seem very simple until you have an argument.

Two child characters. It's 5 am. The entire set a bed. They discover their deceased Granddad's effects under the bed and play with them. They 'phone' Granddad to check it's OK – he says, 'Yes, as long as you don't use my spectacles'. They play, they fall out. They make up. They realise that, if they don't make up, they can't actually continue playing. They play again – but this time making up the story with the audience as they go along, using the 'Dramatic Story-Building' technique described earlier – every performance is different. As well as friendship, this play is about the joys of sharing make-believe together.

It also touches on bereavement. We had been told death was a taboo subject, but by then Guy and I had watched our four year-old daughter say goodbye to my mother's corpse. Our younger daughter at age five had given a present of her drawing to my father on his deathbed, and it was the subject of his last smile. Death isn't taboo. Little children are very straightforward about death – it happens. They begin to get screwed up about it, if adults are not honest with them about it, and they are not included in the ritual of honouring a dead person.

Plays about Family Relationships

Quicksilver then began what became a trilogy about family relationships. Family bonds have the greatest impact on little children. My eldest two children argued and fought a lot. The arrival of my third child brought the arrival of a new baby centre-stage, and I decided to visit sibling rivalry. This time for my research I went to a mother and babies drop-in playgroup, and to families in their own homes. Plenty of examples of three and four year olds usurped by their mewling and puking newly-born baby brother or sister. I saw a lot of cuddling and love towards their babies, but I also saw the wretchedness on their faces, and a sly pinch. Even a little girl who threw sand into a strange new baby's pram. Othello's got nothing on the monstrous jealousy of the new big brother or sister!

Baby Love: What a relief then for children to see exactly these worst feelings in someone else. The main character was Harry, on his own in his bedroom at night-time. He's really excited about the new baby; it's going to be really, really great. The baby arrives and it is great for about thirty seconds. The audience switches all its attention to the baby, leaving Harry feeling murderous with jealousy. He is horrible to her, and they fight a lot. Finally, however, when she is in real physical danger, he feels the need to protect his sibling, and so a bond is formed. This play spoke across cultures, playing the UK, Mexico, Japan and Singapore.

All By My Own: Loss, fear and anger in a series of stories in suitcases, the literal and emotional baggage of a woman on a train on her way to make peace with her daughter, and connect with her granddaughter. The audience were her fellow passengers on a train. Children found the anger of the small child not being listened to, the funniest thing, as a torrent of angry words and accusations were directed at the guilty adult.

The Mamas and the Papas: The frustration with parents taken one step further. Parent and child swap roles. In asking the child to empathise with the adult, and the adult to empathise with the child, it gave the children a taste of power, and gave the adults food for thought.

I had learnt much up to this point. Small children like and need:

- small shows with small audiences in small spaces, in small amounts, at the right time of day, about things that matter to them
- simple direct language, which can be poetic e.g. 'he got up, and left a warm shadow on the bed'
- the truth, delivered sensitively to draw them in, rather than terrify them

Some theatre makers would argue that they don't need story, and how can we presume to give them stories of adult making. One reason I believe children like story is this – between the ages of three and four they begin to distinguish between pretend and real. At three they play quite quietly. At four or five they begin to add a running commentary to their play, they begin to sequence events, begin to understand cause and effect. They are on their way to discovering that their actions have consequences, and therefore they have responsibilities.

Another bone of contention among theatre-makers is the old chestnut about adults playing children. Children accept this is an actor playing a part. What is an issue is actors playing the stereotype of a child – but that's just bad acting.

Research into Child Creativity

In 2000, the Department of Education introduced an Early Years Curriculum: personal, social and emotional development; communication, language and literacy; mathematical knowledge development; knowledge and understanding of the world; physical development – and creative development. This government initiative resulted in many requests for workshops on creativity for teachers, and Early Years practitioners. It was simple to transfer drama and story techniques, but it felt unsatisfactory. What was needed was a change in perception on the part of adults looking after these children, to recognise that play is a creative and intellectual activity.

I began a period of research and development into children's creativity, in order to channel it into a theatre play that could validate children's play as an element for which the children themselves can take credit; and to contribute to teachers' understanding of the value of play as a way of learning. It would offer resource materials for each school in a unique and exciting way. We drew on:

- The Reggio Emilia Child Centre Ethos: developing children's problem-solving, and interpersonal skills
- Vivian Gussin Paley's Storytelling/Story-Acting Approach: facilitating the making of stories by children
- Dorothy Heathcote. Drama-in-Education. Archetypal props. We assembled a box of things: bowl, candle, chest, cloak, coffin, cup, fire, flower, key, ring, sheath, sword, staff, star, and water.

Children performing in a play of their own

The following year I decided not to lead or direct the children and to keep the materials as simple as possible. In a cleared corner of the room I placed boxes, in which were cardboard tubes, fabrics of various size, colour and texture, washing line and pegs, and a big roll of paper. There was also some rope, gaffa tape, masking tape and felt pens. I wanted to simply let the children unpack what was there and play with it. 'There is some stuff over there you might like to have a look at and play with. There's one thing I need you to remember, if there is any pretend fighting, it's important not to actually hurt anyone. Remember – no one must get hurt, by accident or on purpose'. With this one simple rule in mind they set to unpack... to begin with there was a flurry of activity, they couldn't believe they had permission to do anything they liked with the materials. The nursery staff were asked to hold back as much as possible from interposing views, contributing to the action, or intervening to discipline the children.

The theatre practitioner in me wanted to find an opportunity for performance in all of this. From the torrent of scenarios that each group produced, I was able to observe and note the emerging themes of their play. I then wrote a short story, drawing together all the major themes that had emerged. When I explained to them that it would be nice to act out the story, they knew immediately what the casting was, and what they had to do. After a short rehearsal, they were able to present their 'play', and have the satisfaction of gaining an audience's attention and praise. This confirmed that children are hugely creative people, who can create worlds out of nothing in their play.

An Open-ended Play

The whole experience gave me the confidence to create a play using open-ended play materials, and try to be as creative as the children. Furthermore we would give the set and props to the children to enable them to develop their own imaginative skills, and let the early years practitioners realise that these children were more creative than they ever could have believed! The next step was to take the same process into the rehearsal room. Actor Anthony Best and I spent a week discovering the potential of play with cloth, cardboard, natural and recycled materials, around the theme of 'upstairs in the sky' – a phrase from the mouth of a four year old. This phrase, which became the title, embodied the open-ended potential for the content as well as the form of the show. Guy Holland and I then created a broad outline for a script which we took into rehearsal to develop through improvisation. Collaboration, the essential quality of improvisation, became a strong theme in the play.

The story box

Upstairs In The Sky: A multi-layered play, a central theme being that trust and acceptance leads to collaboration, which can generate creativity, pleasure and emotional well-being. Two delivery people, 'him' and 'her', enter the classroom whilst the children are gathered on the carpet, singing. The delivery people comically debate whether this is the right place, the children's attention is caught and the play has begun. The teacher confirms they are in the right place, and the delivery people bring in a large cardboard box.

The box is the 'Make it Yourself Story Kit', and clearly belongs to all the children as the delivery note lists all their names. The note also instructs the delivery people to 'install' the Kit: 'use anything in the box in any way you like to make a story'. Music accompanies the performance. This is their first challenge. He doesn't do stories – She however likes nothing better than to make stories and have fun. They tentatively reveal the box's contents – beautiful pieces of fabric in a range of colours and textures, several boxes nesting inside each other, card-board tubes, cotton wool, silver foil, recycled and natural materials, twigs, cones.

'Him' and 'Her' as Storytellers. They succeed in using the materials to tell their separate stories – one tells the story of *Little Red Riding Hood*, the other tells *Snow White* – but they fail to collaborate. They try to ignore each other, and then begin to take each other's props to tell their own story. It ends in a loud argument. Audiences sometimes shout out, and tell them to play together, be kind, share, and tell the same story. Other audiences quietly wait for the characters to sort themselves out; theatre should tap into the whole emotional experience for the audience. She begins to resolve the conflict by weaving the stories of *Snow White* and *Little Red Riding Hood*

They argue

together. By accepting his story She accepts Him and He in response contributes to, and concludes their joint story. A sense of mutual trust is established and, after apologising to each other, they agree to try again.

Loss as a Theme. With generosity towards each other, they create the story of Princess Veronica and her grandfather King Jim, much loved but very old. The title *Upstairs in the Sky* suggested death as another theme. At the end of a long life, King Jim disappears 'upstairs in the sky' into a beautiful cloudscape. His granddaughter Princess Veronica is worried about him, and goes to find him. He tells her that he is safe and happy, and he won't be coming home... some things change. But of course some things remain the same, his love for her will be as strong as it ever was, forever, and she can always revisit him in her memory. Reassured, she returns to everyday life, confident that she is loved and remembered.

This second theme of loss and bereavement is sensitively presented, so that any child (or adult) who has experienced the death of someone close can empathise. For those children who have not experienced bereavement, they will recognise a sense of loss and separation, responding to it in their own way. Research suggests that children can suffer enormous damage if not supported in grief, and it is essential to recognise death as a real issue. The response to this theme has been very positive, proof that perhaps UK attitudes are becoming more open to discussing death. Hurray!

Being Brave. The third theme of the play combines being brave and trying something new. Princess Veronica has to brave a dark staircase to reach her grandfather's room at the top of a tall tower. Her eyes adjust to the dark, and she becomes more confident. When confronted with an invitation to cross a silver bridge into the cloudscape, where she might find out what has happened to her beloved grandfather, she realises that if she doesn't try, she'll never know. With the confidence she has gained from meeting her grandfather, she strides out to meet another day, and a life without him.

The delivery people get a call on their mobile phone and leave, amidst smiles and goodbyes. 'One Make-it-Yourself-Story-Kit. Delivered and installed. It's all yours now to play with, and have lots of fun.' The stage remains, set in the final tableau of cloudscape and sunrise, enticing the children to come and touch, explore, remove, rebuild, reenact or do whatever they want to do with these materials. Children always want to explore set and props after a performance, and finally here is a show that not only allows, but also invites the children to do this. They respond immediately and enthusiastically, play for as long as their teachers will let them.

The children have engaged creatively in watching the show, sharing their imaginations and their emotions with their peers and the actors, in consensual belief in the story and the 'props'. For example – a cone of cardboard with a lollipop stuck in the top of it is Princess Veronica – a piece of cotton wool is a cat from a cloudscape world. They have witnessed and been part of a simple yet complex experience that has stimulated them intellectually and emotionally.

The Big Pretend

The parallel between theatre rehearsal and devising and children's play, is strong. Theatre is play, it is the 'big pretend' shared between players, or between players and audience. Watching children's play can be boring; it can take a very long time before you realise what the play theme is. Similarly, in theatre, to satisfy an audience simply to play is not enough, the play needs to be set in context – this can be narrative, or in more experiential pieces it can be visual and audio vocabulary. Either way, it confirms what we began with at that inaugural theatre for the Under-5's Conference in 1989 – 'the infant mind is closer to the bare rudiments of theatre, poetry and art, than are our cluttered adult minds…'

Carey English is Joint Director of Quicksilver Theatre with Guy Holland.

SPECIAL NEEDS AUDIENCES

Tim Webb explains how the Oily Cart company became involved in this area, the development of their techniques, and the links to theatre for all children.

How we began

Oily Cart successfully performed for pre-school children in play centres and nurseries, with the support of staff and parents. Then in 1988 the head of a school for young people with Severe Learning

Pre-school child audience

Disabilities saw one of our sessions. He invited us to perform one of our Under-5's shows to his young people – some of whom were as old as eighteen. In my previous incarnation as an actor in TIE teams I had experience of theatre for people with learning disabilities. I was sure that although a young person with a learning disability, might have intellectual ability similar to a child's, their interests, and aspirations would be quite different. We suggested we do some research, and create a piece, age-appropriate and truly relevant to the young people in his school. We visited Special Schools across London. Again and again we were told that it was essential to take time in work for this audience. Our standard 45 to 60 minute show was of little use. They would benefit from interacting with us over a longer period, but gain little from sitting as passive spectators.

Research

We saw for ourselves that the students had a wide range of abilities (some were highly verbal, others not at all, some were mobile, others confined to wheelchairs, some sighted, some not, some with hearing, others with none at all) and that no one type of performance would be appropriate for all of them. We came to the conclusion that we needed an interactive, flexible form of theatre in which the performers could adapt the action to suit the needs of any young person with Severe Learning Disabilities (SLD) with whom they found themselves working. After this brief period of research, we devised our first piece for young people with learning disabilities.

Box of Socks (1988): A trio of beings from outer space have crashed their flying saucer into the school. These aliens have to be instructed in all aspects of life on earth by the young people in the school. For me, the highlight was to be taken on a trip around the local shops with a group of older pupils, who spent much of their time persuading their alien companion that it was no use demanding pork chops in the newsagents, or a three-piece suit in the builders' merchants. The show lasted a whole school day, comprised of several modules, each one pitched at a different age and/or ability level. The school staff decided which student should join which module. Frequently, the same students would show up in two or three different modules (being suited to one by age, another by verbal language ability and a third by mobility).

Between 1989 and 1992, we created four new productions for SLD schools, each touring widely around the UK and obviously answering an enormous demand. There were other companies doing very valuable work in this sector, especially the Leeds-based Interplay. Schools were avid for theatre (and other art forms) of good quality that was truly responsive to the needs of their young people.

'I had a momentary frisson of sheer disbelief that the company would be capable of reaching them (the students with Profound and Multiple Learning

Disabilities) in any way. I could not have been more wrong. The whole was a triumph of joy, faith and optimism, and you felt privileged to see it.'

Times Educational Supplement

Georgie Goes To Hollywood (1994): Georgie arrives in school determined to make a feature film as cheaply as possible. The students are recruited as cast, extras, musicians, scenic artists and sound-effects specialists, and each scene of the film-in-progress is allotted to one of five groups, based on ability level.

For the two day long programmes like *Georgie Goes To Hollywood*, the pupils worked in age-related groups, and a Profound and Multiple Learning Disability (PMLD) group. It was clear this group had the least alternative provision. We decided to concentrate on the challenge of creating accessible theatre for them. Theatre for people with learning disabilities is a quagmire of impenetrable acronyms (PMLD, ASD, SLD) and categories that often seem designed to deny the potential of the young people shoved into them. The best that can be said about these terms and definitions is that they provide a crude shorthand understood by the families, schools, and the artists working with them.

PMLD

People with a multiplicity of disabilities – sensory, intellectual and physical impairments. This group often have mobility problems and use little or no verbal language, although they may communicate using signs, signals or objects of reference. Many need help in feeding, dressing and toileting and they remain at an early developmental level, requiring one-to-one support throughout their lives. From the point of view of the parents, the families, the teachers and the carers of people with PMLD, the complex nature of the impairment means that trips out are fraught with difficulties. Is there wheelchair access? Will suitable toileting facilities be available? Will there be a hoist? Where could medication be administered? Visits to the theatre or cinema can result in complaints from people offended by the involuntary noises made by people with PMLD.

We came to believe that in the short term the audiences with PMLD urgently needed appropriate work of high quality, delivered in an environment with all necessary facilities. For the most part, that meant taking specialist PMLD work into Special Schools.

Tickled Pink (1996): This piece drew together our experience of work with people with PMLD. It was a turning-point in the development of the company. It forced us to scrutinise every aspect of our theatre practice. None of the usual norms of theatre could be accepted without question. Some participants may be sighted, but others not; some may have good hearing, others may have no hearing at all. In short, it was pointless to have a show that relied on the old theatrical stand-bys of seeing and hearing. Most theatre is still about a group of people at one end of a room, looking at a smaller group of people at the other end of the room. If some of the audience can't hear and others can't see, this is not an effective model of theatre for them. Some of the PMLD audience will have long and short-term memory, but others will not. Some will have a good understanding of cause and effect, readily appreciating that if I drop this cup it will smash on the floor; others will make no such assumption. Therefore, we have to carefully examine some of the usual ideas about narrative and theatre. If some of the audience are unable to remember what happened at the beginning of a show, we need to examine our notions of plot, character development and story resolution.

What is *Tickled Pink*? It is a state of being. It can be a waft of air from a fan or down the bore of a clarinet; the scent of a rose petal, or the touch of velvet; enclosed and secure spaces saturated in colour and heaped with soft-scented pillows. It's a drama but there's no story…

'It's something to do with the people in the team, their endless research and the way in which they give the children time to respond,' says Sarah Melman, senior teacher at Jack Tizzard School for children with Severe Learning Disabilities.

Hammocking

Some of the people with whom we work may not be sighted, or hearing. Our theatre needed to involve the other senses, especially touch and smell, but also the kinaesthetic sense, the sense that the body has of its own movement in space. We needed to make a truly multi-sensory theatre. We investigated massage, aroma-therapy and hammocking – we would literally swing the participants in a hammock between two performers. Fanning and low range sound creating vibrations accessible even to those with no hearing.

Secondly, because there will be a range of likes and dislikes, we needed to make theatre that was highly interactive and adaptable to the requirements of any individual. In *Tickled Pink*, a team of four Oily Cart performers worked with groups of approximately twenty young people with PMLD (an equal number of carers was present). Helped by the carers, our performers could modulate their performance to have the maximum effect on each participant. Each performer was free to choose from a range of options when working with an individual. For example, if someone was reacting badly to the introduction of a new stimulus (say – fanning) then the performer had the option of re-introducing something, (say – a chime) that had been effective before.

The Role of Companions

Teachers, care assistants, family members accompanying the young people through these experiences, was vital. It can be difficult with particular individuals to interpret their body language and other ways of communication. A twist of the head can be a way of indicating delight, and another's way of communicating apprehension. So the performers had to remain aware of the companions' responses. On the other hand, experienced performers can sometimes take the companions' reactions with a pinch of salt. Definitions applied to young people with learning disabilities can be reductive and prevent us seeing the potential within an individual; so too, carers sometimes may make limiting assumptions. One of the most delightful aspects is when a young person with complex needs, given the focus and the intensity of a performance, suddenly displays an ability, or a side of their personality, not seen before.

'We saw reactions from pupils that were amazing! For example a tactile defensive pupil reaching out for a balloon and volunteering his hand for a massage! And pupils refraining from self-injurious behaviour whilst on the magic carpet ride – smiling and interacting.'

East Shore School, Portsmouth.

The main problem with *Tickled Pink* was numbers. Even with the help of carers, four performers seemed thinly spread among twenty young people with PMLD. The more passive young people tended to receive less attention than the energetic and demanding. We began to consider the artistic – and the economic – issues of moving toward a one-to-one performance model.

Hunky Dory (1998): We took the risk that schools might find the cost of one-to-one work uneconomic and launched a show in which four performers and a stage manager worked into an installation, representing an underground chamber, with a maximum of five young people (and five companions) for each fifty-minute long session. The schools showed no hesitation in booking the piece, even though we could only work with a maximum of twenty young people per day. When questioned, teachers and carers were clear that the quality of the pupils' experience was paramount, and that they could readily see that one-on-one work would make a greater impression. *Hunky Dory* explored the world underground; the textures, aromas, visual delights of clay, sand, crystal, roots and water. We introduced the didgeridoo, and the double bass to our repertoire of deep and resonating sounds.

A Learning Disabled Actor

For half the tour we also introduced Mark Foster, an amazing performer. Mark had been educated entirely within Severe Learning Disability Schools, but as a teenager he became part of Razor Edge, a training scheme for theatre practitioners with a learning disability, directed by Irene Kappes and Mike Ormerod. The low notes of the didgeridoo were perfectly complemented by Mark's phenomenally deep voice but more importantly he brought an intense empathy and commitment to the work. He has worked with us on productions every year since *Hunky Dory*, and apart from his talent, we believe that he acts as a role model for many of the young people. In Autumn 2004, he was cast in *Hippity Hop*, not one of our shows for SLD audiences, but a production for children under four years old.

The Water Experience

We had often seen that some young people were at their most relaxed when floating in the warmth of a hydrotherapy pool. Here their bodies, so often confined in splints, corsets and wheelchairs, could float freely, the effects of gravity ameliorated by the supporting water.

A thought began to grow – if we added music, lighting, fountains, sprays, mists, bubbles and perfumes to the hydro pool environment, and if our performers worked in our, now usual, multi-sensory, close-up and highly interactive way, perhaps we could enhance the water experience.

Big Splash (1999): The first of a trilogy of hydro pool-based productions between 1999 and 2001. We worked with two young people in the water. A musician played at close quarters as the two participants were taken on avoyage around the pool on our Bubble Boats, supportive

The water experience

vessels, apparently made of translucent bubbles. Meanwhile, the next two students were being gently introduced to the experience that lay ahead by two performers animating a pavilion of delights set up close to the poolside.

Trampoline

Each of the shows in the *Big Splash* trilogy had moments of intense beauty and elicited astonishing and delightful reactions, and I am sure that we will return to water-based work in the future. As 2001 came to an end, we began to explore another medium for bringing movement to people with great mobility impairment – the trampoline. We were greatly assisted in the development of this work by Eddie Anderson, a retired Special School head, who has pioneered a unique approach in the use of trampolines by people with complex disabilities.

The young person will be sitting or lying on the trampoline, looked after by a minimum of two performers. As music plays, the performers and their trampoline guest can generate a vast range of movement from the trampoline bed. The movement can be gentle and relaxing, or it can be made tremendously exhilarating, depending on the requirements of the young person bouncing with you. In many respects the experience is similar to that in the hydro pool; there is a range of movement denied to many young people on the ground, and sometimes, delightfully, people who spend their lives usually strapped in wheelchairs, find themselves soaring, free of the effects of gravity.

Boing! (2002): Here we invited our young guests to join us in a mysterious, Middle Eastern night spot, an inflatable pleasure palace filled with perfumes, musical delights – and at the heart of all this, the legendary Flying Carpet (a thinly disguised trampoline.)

Moving Pictures (2003): We kept the nightclub setting and the Flying Carpet ride, but added pre-recorded and live projected video. Many young people with complex needs have issues with self-image and body awareness. Video proved to be an invaluable tool in enhancing our participants' awareness of their own experience. As they bounced on the Flying Carpet and we sang out their names, they could see their own faces, projected live on the screen above. Many showed tremendous delight on seeing their own giant image and finding themselves at the centre of everyone's attention. The highlights of each participant's experience were edited onto a tape left with each venue. In many cases these tapes are played back over and over again, so the experience can be re-lived. The effect of our work resonates long after the live performance.

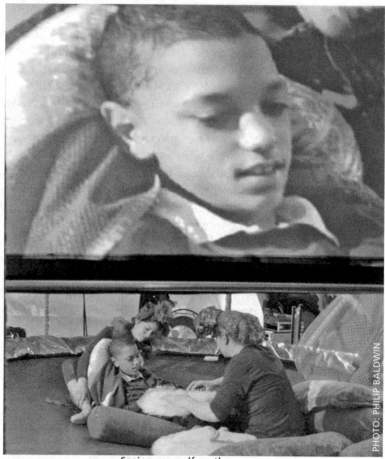

PHOTO: PHILIP BALDWIN

Seeing yourself on the screen

Pre- and Post-show Activities

We are convinced that when it comes to working with an audience of young people with PMLD, the more actual live theatre performance can be prefigured with video, print, links to our website, work packs with suggested pre- and post-show activities, the more the young people will gain from the experience. Ideally, we would spend a week, a month, a term working with each of our PMLD audiences but as this is impractical, the best way to extend the footprint of our work is to help the schools and other venues to prepare for and follow up performances. The performances get the greatest reactions, when a school has structured a whole term's work around an Oily Cart visit.

ASD

One group who cannot be defined as PMLD are people who are said to have a low functioning type of Autistic Spectrum Disorder (ASD). Frequently, these young people are mobile, but may have difficulty with the full development of verbal language, display rigid patterns of behaviour, dislike change, have issues in relating to other people and understanding that others may not think as they do. For them the visit of a theatre company, strangers transforming the school hall and indulging in role play could be the worst of experiences. People with ASD often find the multi-layered and attention-demanding kind of PMLD work to be an assault on their senses. We created a version of our forthcoming PMLD production, *Conference of the Birds* specifically tailored to audiences with Autistic Spectrum Disorder.

Conference of the Birds: After a period of research we adopted three strategies to make our work suitable for an audience with ASD.

1. We made *Conference of the Birds* clearly structured. It is introduced by a video trailer of the episode to come, with a definite beginning, middle and end. Between the episodes there would be a pause, silence and space. Also before the visit they would have a large photo book containing the social story of the show.
2. In Special Schools a simple activity, for example, how to eat in public, is deconstructed, so that people with ASD, who often have problems knowing how to behave in social situations, learn the socially-acceptable pattern of behaviour. Our Social Story deconstructed a theatre company visiting a school, introducing the characters and themes, indicating the action and even the audience's possible reactions to this, doing everything possible to demystify the whole event for young people who find strangers and new situations hard to handle.
3. We invited each member of the audience to sit in one of our six Leaf Chairs for the performance. These cocoon-like chairs are suspended from a frame that allows them to be bounced, twisted, swayed and spun. They are fabulously comfortable and yet can also, like a

trampoline, be used to generate all sorts of kinaesthetic pleasures. Our spectators, with or without ASD, love them. *Conference of the Birds* has been extremely well received by school, families, and the young people and we shall be touring it again in 2005.

'Every once in a while one discovers a theatre show so special, so beautifully crafted and so emotionally affecting that one feels simply privileged to have experienced it. Conference of the Birds ... is such a production.'

Mark Brown, Sunday Herald

Transferring these Techniques to Theatre for all Children

At the end of the 1990's, our shows for the very young tended to be very much of the sit-down-and-watch variety. Then as we began to see how the interactive and multi-sensory work we were doing in Special Schools would engage audiences, commonly defined as being hard-to-reach, it dawned on us that similar approaches might be relevant to the very young.

Knock! Knock! Who's There?: Here we created installations where our young audiences walked through the fourth wall into the world of our play, where they would find stimuli for all five senses, and actively engage with the characters.

'Storytelling performance for the under fives and their carers. Touchy-feely, scratch-and-touch. It is a total delight. It is not often that theatre makes you feel blessed out. But this miniature does in part because the audience – small though it is in every way – is made to feel an active participant.'

Lyn Gardner, The Guardian

Jumpin' Beans: For children under four. There were two distinct versions of the show. One was for children from two to four years old, and while multi-sensory and interactive, was plot-driven and reliant on a good deal of spoken language. The other was for children between six months and two years-old and their parents, and was much less dependent on verbal language, conjuring a succession of beautiful moments to engage each different sense of its very young audience and their companions.

We were astonished at the reception of the six months to two year-old's version of *Jumpin' Beans*. When we first began preparations for this, we had assumed it would be about leading the parents through a sort of theatricalised play session, in which we provided a lovely setting, props, music and a series of cues to facilitate their play with their children. In fact, as soon as we began to workshop this version, it was startlingly apparent that the babies and the toddlers themselves were our primary audience – they had been gripped by this non-verbal non-linear, and multi-sensory piece, in their own right.

'The responses were wonderful, in fact many of the staff were moved to tears by the way the pupils responded. All were totally engaged throughout – a very difficult thing to achieve with learners with such complex needs.'

Powys School, Wrexham

Future Plans

Oily Cart will continue to develop its work for audiences with PMLD and ASD and, if our history is anything to go by, we will discover even more strategies for engaging this often neglected audience. We plan new approaches to include the school staff and parents in the preparation and follow-up of our live performances. When *Conference of the Birds* returns to the repertoire in the Spring of 2005, the tour will open with three two-day long training sessions at three regional centres, involving up to ninety Special School teachers, members of the Equals Consortium.

We will also increase the involvement of performers with a learning disability, like Mark Foster. In 2004's *Conference of the Birds*, he was joined for the first time by another actor with a learning disability, Housni Hassan, who shares Mark's empathy for the young people with complex needs, and his enormous commitment to the work. Their successful partnership has convinced us of the need to develop a second Oily Cart company – a team of performers with learning disabilities, who, supported by personal assistants and members of the Oily Cart technical team, would deliver their own version of the Oily Cart interactive, multi-sensory theatre. Fundraising has begun and we hope to launch this second Oily Cart team in late 2005.

Most of our productions for people with PMLD and ASD have been performed in schools, but we are planning to do much more of this kind of work in integrated settings – and especially with family groups.

As we develop our work, we must not lose sight of the fact that our main aim is to bring stimulation and delight to young people with whom it is very difficult to communicate. The Oily Cart performers have an advantage: all too often the school staff, even the families of these young people, necessarily have to deal with them in a very utilitarian way – feeding, changing, washing and so on. The Oily Cart attempts nothing as useful as all that. Our role is to bring these audiences gratuitous pleasure – surely they can't have enough of that.

Tim Webb co-founded Oily Cart Theatre, and has written over twenty playscripts.

THEATRE FOR EMOTIONALLY-DISTURBED CHILDREN

Peter Rumney recounts the formation of Dragon Breath making theatre with, and for, angry children in an angry world.

How can we make a piece of theatre that truly reflects and connects with the lives of my young audience...? How can the audience make significant contributions to the development of our production...? What can I learn as an artist from the young people I am working with? How can they inspire me as a creator...? How can we reach out to children who find life in school so difficult that they normally miss out on contact with artists...? How can we, as theatre makers, influence the way teachers think and how schools are run...?

These are the questions that inspired us to embark on the Dream City/Dragon Breath Project. The result was a collaboration between different cultural partners, that turned freelance artists into producers and managers.

Working with Angry Children

To begin, as the poet says, at the beginning. Made 2 Measure Workshops, a Nottingham-based collective of theatre practitioners, and educators, has been developing innovative programmes of work with primary school children (aged 5 to 11) who have what our education system calls 'emotional and behavioural difficulties'. They are the children who are at risk of isolating themselves, or being isolated from their school community, or of being denied (because they are so challenging) opportunities to find the very voice that could express the turmoil and confusion of their lives.

Participatory Arts Workshop

A writer, director, scenographer, musician, choreographer and an actor are gathered in the school hall, enclosed by swirls of corrugated cardboard walls that create an organic, focused, calm space. Ten children aged 5 to 10, and their teacher, are invited into the space. Ritual stones are carried into the room... a drum begins to speak... a huge collaborative painting begins... The children begin work on a variety of creative activities that cater for multiple intelligences and different learning styles. The adult team is always diverse in term of ethnicity, age, gender and so on. Positive role modelling is key to the work. Most importantly, the adults participate alongside the children in the activities. We want to offer creative pathways for the children and to enable their teachers and peers to see them in a different, more positive light to build their confidence in expressing themselves.

We believe passionately that, as theatre makers, our role is to give witness to the experiences of our audience, and to challenge their preconceptions about themselves and the world around them. Over the years many powerful and challenging stories have been shared, hinted or guessed at. We wanted to turn these stories and relationships into a piece of theatre that would reflect not only the lives of children struggling to cope, but of all children – after all, anger, loss, disappointed trust, hope and aspiration affect us all.

Extracts from the Diary of making *Dragon Breath*

Week 1: The Residency

Around the school hall, small groups of children and adults are making sculptural Dream catchers, and discussing the emotions trapped within the Dream catchers. After a morning of music, dance, painting and games, the pupils are creating their own worlds, safe places, dreamscapes. A seven year old boy is working alongside the Choreographer, Liz Clark. They have built up a relationship during the course of the morning. They are constructing a sculptural Dream catcher. Liz asks what the sculpture is to be. 'It's a Dragon', says the boy. No one is aware of it yet, but a central image of the play has been created.

We are trying to discover what the ideas, concerns and feelings of the children are. Although the theme of the play is difficult emotions and relationships, the creative team do not bring a set of fixed ideas or scenarios to the process. There is as yet no title, no genre, no certainties. We want to explore dreams, because dreams are a safe way to examine emotions with our young audience.

Now we are about to make discoveries with the children.
– One girl refuses to speak. She shouts if she cannot keep the drum she has been playing. The only word she uses is 'No'.

– A small boy squares up to his cousin belligerently. His face is red with anger. He does not know how to channel his aggression creatively. The class teacher gently restrains him. The boy returns to work.

– A girl works quietly in a corner. A boy hides in the folds of the cardboard wall that envelops the hall.

We want to explore a medieval or early renaissance setting for the play. Three characters are revealed to the children one by one. The pupils immediately respond to and empathise with a Knight searching for his brother… a Prisoner locked in a dungeon… a lonely Young Man seeking friends. These characters have been altered by contact with the children earlier in the day. The 'characters' in the room are shaping the 'characters' in the play.

Overnight, Peter Rumney has written poems and speeches for the actors, based on the previous day's observations, interactions, and pupils' responses to the characters. He decides to experiment with dramatic verse form to see how children with very limited experience of theatre and poetry, indeed children for whom communication is itself an issue, respond to the language.

> **Albert:** I like the night
> Quite quiet
> Silent
> On my own
> No one to interrupt my thoughts
> No one
> No one, I am no one
> Empty.

The director, Rosamunde Hutt, scenographer Nettie Scriven, and writer have been creating a laboratory in which to explore the characters. The characters are revealed (through the poetic texts) to the children. The pupils are invited to enter into role with the characters, to support and question them. The children seem to take over. Four children go to 'Albert', and try to comfort him.

The children each draw a character as they understand him/her… they are invited to express not just the representational image but the emotional life of the character. A girl draws 'John' behind bars. For actor Andrea Davy these bars have so far been internalised… the child has intuited the actor's process and generates another important image in the future production...

An autistic child, who rarely speaks and con-stantly runs around the hall, offers his insight into the emotional state of a character through a sketched drawing. Finally, the group build an environment that is 'Albert's' home. The creative team will later use the image of this as a starting point to explore where the character will 'live' in the play and how this reflects his psychological state.

Children comfort Albert

The children act out the various characters, responding to that which most nearly reflects how they feel and a rich resource is created, from which all the creative team can draw image, text, sound – and inspiration.

Week 2: Try Out in School

The audience awaits. The mournful sound of bells rings out around the school hall. From behind the waiting children a three metre high set of steps is wheeled slowly through the space. At its summit a Knight is perched, singing: 'The Dragon... the Dragon... I see the Dragon... the Enemy... fly towards the City...' The Jester enters. The genre of fairy tales has been adopted and subverted, turned upside down. A familiar yet challenging world picture is to be presented to the children. A dragon flies into and destroys the twin towers of a medieval city –

the theme of anger, and how to deal with it, has found its embodiment in the piece.

Queen: (*Sung*) Lost. Lost.
My daughter's lost
In the sandstorm dust
And now I count the cost

The creative team has devised a set of questions and tasks that must be answered over the next three days – Does the story engage? Do we need to simplify? Does the language work? Are the forms challenging? Are they too challenging? Can we enable the children to express their understanding of the characters' predicaments? Are the characters and situations authentic? Will the children be stimulated to express their feelings of hurt, anger and disappointment through painting and movement?

A troubled ten year-old girl has painted a lifesize self-portrait of 'Me as a Dragon'. She is working with a student, trying to create a movement piece that grows out of the painting. But when it is time for everyone to share their dances, she loses confidence and shrinks back from the group. A senior member of the team crawls over to her

The performance

on all fours and asks: 'Shall I dance it for you? Will you help me... help me show everyone your dance?' They both begin to create physically the dragon she has drawn. The scenographer and her team of design students are noting the colour of the Dragon's wings, and sketching the image.

A surly eight year-old puts on his hand the glove puppet that has been mocked up to represent a Baby Dragon. He talks in role to the Baby Dragon's friend, now re-named 'Alberto': 'I'm angry so I'm going to spit fire. Can't stop me. I want to find my Mum. Alberto you can run away with me, from my Mum, she's spiteful. You can fly on my back... Why doesn't the King come and see me any more?'

Finally, at the end of the residency, we ask the children how the play should end. Can they offer endings for a play about anger and 'behaviour' that are challenging without being moralistic, hopeful without being simplistic? How would they problem-solve the causes of the vengeance and violence that characterise our world?

Performance of the play

The Jester invites the audience to move from one side of the traverse stage to the other, as the action of the play moves inside the medieval city. Here, and later in the play, we shift the audience, we ask them to promenade in order to move their bodies, avoid restlessness and, thematically, view the unfolding characters and action from another 'perspective'. Theatre, the most multiple of art forms, is here exploring the audience's 'kinetic intelligence'. Many challenging pupils, children who might not have been expected to last five minutes watching a piece of static live theatre, are engrossed for an hour and a half.

After the performance a boy stands up and says to Bad Boy Alberto: 'You are not a 'bad boy'... you are a good boy... have courage...'

Post-performance workshops

Throughout the development process of *Dragon Breath*, the images, themes, experiences, emotions, music making, movement and stories of the participating pupils have been the inspiration for the text, design and other production elements. For us, the play is then validated by the reactions of the children to the performance. We discover, from the workshops and the subsequent residencies, that the audience have a deep understanding and empathy with the predicament of stage characters who were originally inspired by the creativity of children themselves. We have created a virtuous circle of artistic endeavour. It empowers the audience members by reflecting their lives authentically. And by presenting this material to teachers (through the production and through the accompanying participatory work), there is an opportunity for adults to value the children they work with differently, and to see them in a new light.

The Birth of Dragon Breath Theatre Company

The project was conceived by myself, as writer, and Joint Director, Nettie Scriven as scenographer. For many years our work with children with 'emotional and behavioural difficulties', had been lauded and encouraged, but funded on a relative shoestring. Three primary schools participated in the development of the script and production design. By the end of the project, we have suddenly become, not just artists and project managers pursuing an idea, but theatre producers and employers engaged in creating and managing a large and high profile production.

> *'Dear all, Thank you for letting us see your play. I sometimes feel like the big dragon when I'm angry, especially when my mum laughs at me. I also feel a bit lonely sometimes. I can't help what I do to people when I'm angry. I am sorry for what I have done.'*
>
> Primary School pupil

> *'It was ace. The part I liked the best was when the Knight rode in on his horse. Sometimes I feel like a big dragon. I feel lost and lonely when my friends ignore me. Yours sincerely, Jack.'*

The company now known as Dragon Breath Theatre was born.

Peter Rumney is a Joint Artistic Director of Dragon Breath Theatre.

8. THEATRE IN THE COMMUNITY

ASIAN THEATRE – YOUNG AUDIENCE AND WRITERS

Dominic Rai relates the development of Mán Melá Theatre community and how it found its audience and new writers.

Telling Untold Stories

For Mán Melá telling British Asian Stories was the beginning – and is still an integral part of our work. In Flanders, there is a memorial to the men from India who fought for the British in the First World War. Seeing the names of hundreds of Indian soldiers including Hindu, Muslim, Sikh and Buddhist, hit home, as their contribution was not known to me, despite having studied World War One at school. Across *The Black Waters* (1998) adapted by Gerald Wells and myself from Mulk Raj Anand's novel, reached a large diverse audience, Asian and non-Asian. There was a need to hear this story. A National Theatre producer saw it and commented on the commitment of the cast. They had to be committed – having failed to secure public funds, the company had to dig deep into their own pockets to stage the three-week run!

PHOTO: DOUGLAS MCBRIDE

The Black Waters

However this project gave us our aims and identity:

- we were committed to telling 'untold stories'
- we aimed to reach a large and diverse audience

Asian Theatre for a Young Audience

It was with *The Cornershop* (2001), a triple bill developed with three new writers that the company found its audience of young British Asians. For me, one of the motives was to explore contemporary Asian experience/identity. We ended up with more than that. Choosing the writers to work with was the easy bit – supporting and mentoring them over a two year period proved to be a challenging experience for all at Mán Melá. The writers were Ravi Mangat (a Sikh of East African heritage), Ashok Patel (a Gujarati Hindu from Leicester) and Yasmin Khan (a Muslim woman from Bedford).

PHOTO: DOUGLAS MCBRIDE

The Cornershop

A concept was shared with the writers over meetings where a cast of five would play the three families – Muslim, Hindu and Sikh. The action of each play would take place in a family shop which also doubles as the family home, allowing us to see the world from the family's point of view including inter-generational conflicts. Three locations – a newsagent shop, a mini-market, and a fabric shop.

All three plays had young protagonists. It was important to give the writers the freedom to tell their stories in a personal style, ensuring the action was character-led, even if the writers were dealing with strong issues in the community.

Jeevan Sathi (Life Partner) by Ashok Patel: The story of two young women and the consequences of their relationship. I did not want to censor the writer so we ended up giving as much support as we could. The tenderness shown did not provoke any laughter from the audience. The violence shown by Nathu, an overzealous uncle towards his niece's lover, always created an uncomfortable silence. (This play was developed further and broadcast on BBC Radio Four in 2003.)

Wish by Ravi Mangat: Satnam wants to sell the family shop in order to widen his son's horizons. This gentle and moving play asks whether magic and love can unite to bring about one's dearest desire, as the young man helps himself and his father recover from his mother's death. The audience loved the humour of this play, especially Satnam's habit of reciting famous lines from western films, from James Cagney to James Bond. The touch of the supernatural to deal with difficult customers and problems gave the play a universality. The family could have been from any cultural background.

Resham (Silk) by Yasmin Khan: A hard-hitting piece set in a fabric shop, that provides insight into honour killings in the Pakistani community. A grandfather kills Sameena, his granddaughter, who he believes has disgraced the family by becoming pregnant by an Afro-Caribbean man. The double life that some young people live, came out in this play. Sameena was a young woman who enjoyed her job as an air hostess and had a boyfriend. Yet when she came home, she was expected to follow a stricter code. A line from the grandfather was: 'He's a black man and a Christian, probably a drug-selling thief.' This was said in the Mosque scene where some of the elders were more in tune with young people and the lives they lead.

Despite the presence of Asian Theatre companies, there have been very few Pakistani characters on stage. Yasmin Chan was one of the first, second-generation Muslim women to have a play go on from commissioning to touring. The authenticity of this play came not only from the writer, but also from the Muslim cast. Seeing these characters on stage gave the opportunity for the audience to relate to issues in their own lives.

We toured from Kent to Scotland to enthusiastic audiences. When we reached the Brady Centre in Whitechapel, East London where we had rehearsed, the show had a strong vibe and we sold out.

Community Theatre Programme

This led us to work with young people more directly. Eastside Arts organised a residency which led to working with Summer University and the Brady Centre. This took real life stories from the East End of

London and converted them into the stuff of drama. Out of this came a week of workshops and a performance at the area workshop programme for young people – the Summer University. It was so successful that the young people wanted to continue meeting so The Eastside Young Writers and Performers Group of fifteen to twenty year-olds was formed in 2001. The group is providing opportunities for young people to write and perform in interesting venues alongside established poets and writers. The young people are, in turn, being inspirational to others.

Young Performers Group

There have been theatre visits and the members have had the opportunity to meet playwrights like Shan Khan, whose play *Office* won the Verity Bargate Award, and Gurpreet Bhatti, who has written for *EastEnders* on TV. There is now a manual on writing.

'It is a totally mixed group in terms of background and gender. It is constantly evolving and giving opportunities for young people to perform their writing at high profile events. In every single case, the young people felt their confidence and skills have increased. We use young writers in a multi-media, multi-cultural framework and give young people a voice and a platform. It is not about patronising them.'

Maggie Crosbie, Literature Development Worker of Eastside Arts

Stories not for Telling: Stories were about mobile phone-jacking, the local prostitute scene, drug-dealing and violence in the Whitechapel area. One of the young people wrote about how some Bengali girls, banned from leaving their homes after dark, go into the streets in the middle of the night when their families are asleep. The young writers also created a contemporary version of the famous Kray gangster twins, in a very funny sketch which touched on modern-day gang culture.

Seema's Story: About a pregnant Bengali girl who has an abortion, it was written by a sixteen year-old girl and developed with the group. The was showcased at Summer University, and finally performed alongside professional actors at the Royal Court Theatre. Work within school and college contexts followed, with participants who had no previous experience of drama work or creative-writing.

Stories Not For Texting: Plays the young writers have developed from the dramas behind text messages.

'What struck me instantly was the genuine buzz of interest in the audience as well as the numbers attending. The performances effortlessly tackled very real issues and situations with humour and understanding, proving that theatre can be just as enthralling dealing with the social issues of today, as it can be delivering Shakespeare.'

Abid Hussain, West Midlands Arts

Future Young Audiences

The position of small culturally-diverse companies in the UK over the last ten years is that too much energy has to be channelled into finding resources that are not always forthcoming, despite having a tried and tested product. *The Cornershop,* a show with both critical and audience appeal, did not get a London run. As a small company you have the ability to create work and connect with the audience but not the resources to promote, produce and tour.

Too much of the culturally-diverse work is London-centric, leaving little room in the other major cities to create a regional voice for the younger generation. The future for companies like Mán Melá is to work in partnership with other companies and theatres who have a vested interest in reaching diverse young audiences, using the power of theatre.

Dominic Rai is Director of Mán Melá Theatre Company. Current projects include 'Chilli in your Eyes', a book about the development of British Asian theatre and writing.

LINKING SCHOOLS AND COMMUNITY AUDIENCES

Julie Ward gives the background to Jack Drum Arts 'Theatre of Stealth' where school-based workshops developed into performances for the whole community in a socially welcoming environment.

We are a collective based in rural south-west County Durham. Company members have backgrounds in teaching, community music, young people's theatre, rural touring, theatre design, film and photography and arts work with special needs. This eclectic mix of skills, interests and experience has resulted in a style of theatre for young people that goes beyond the 'tick box' constraints of curriculum-driven theatre for schools, and reaches out to the local community as a whole.

Our Community

Fundamentally important had been the need for us to carve out a niche for ourselves in the community, to create a reputation for delivering high quality accessible theatre, and to create a demand for our work in a locality where there was little professional theatre. We began by making relationships with key partners. Many of these were schools. Mindful of their strategic importance within their communities they were keen to find new ways of engaging with parents as well as pupils. We discovered that within the schools of our rural area there was little movement; settled residents whose families had been around for generations – a small world where everyone knew everyone else, and it was relatively easy to be drawn into the fold. We are an ear for teachers coping with the complexities of current arts-in-education schemes. In the midst of all this, we operate as primary creators, devising new theatre and media projects that we hope our communities will both learn from and enjoy.

From our beginnings in 1986, we had been working in schools delivering workshops and small-scale storytelling theatre projects to mainly top junior school, ten and eleven year olds, and special needs pupils. Then in 1997, things began to change. We started to create work for an adult audience, touring local pubs. *The Bonny Moorhen* was our retelling of a local nineteenth-century leadminers' riot. Known locally as

'The Battle of Stanhope', this uprising against the power of the bishopric almost sparked an English Revolution, occurring between the Battle of Waterloo and the Peterloo Massacre. We gave the story a Brechtian treatment with songs and comic set-pieces to lighten the history. It went down a storm. It won the Guinness Pub Theatre Award, and was likened to *The Cheviot, the Stag and the Black, Black Oil* – the seminal play showing the lives of working-class people by 7.84 Theatre.

The leadminers in rebellion

Linking a School and Community Audience

The Bonny Moorhen: Amongst the audience from the local community who crowded into the smoky backrooms of the Dales' pubs were local teachers. They made us realise the play had an educational potential. When the Arts Council invited proposals for projects to develop New Audiences we successfully submitted the idea of a schools tour of *The Bonny Moorhen* with a three-day workshop programme that preceded the performance.

The workshops were run by playwright and singer/songwriter, Jim Woodland, a local actress and drama worker. Together, they introduced the target secondary school audiences to the local social

PHOTO: HELEN WARD

and political history, through the use of song and role play. The history done, the pupils were then encouraged to create characters who might have been present at the annual Leadminers' Pay Day, a wild affair, more like a carnival than an official procedure. On the day of the performance, the pupils set up their stalls along the entrance ways to the school halls and, in character, entertained, harangued and otherwise engaged their friends and family, as they arrived for the evening's performance. The front two rows were our workshop participants who, relieved of their inhibitions, became an enthusiastic audience, setting the tone for a good night out!

In our analysis of the project, we realised we had stumbled across an excellent formula. Whilst the notion of 'pub theatre' may not seem suitable for a school audience, we had managed to transfer the energy and rumbustiousness of a pub setting to our education work, thereby replicating a familiar atmosphere akin to a working men's club for our non theatre-going audience. Encouraged by their offspring to come along and view the results of our education work – adults became our new audiences too, and enjoyed the local nature of the story!

Extending the Approach

Set in Stone: Two years later, we had the opportunity to create a second piece of adult theatre for schools' touring, inspired by a much more recent event – World War One – and in particular the adding of a name to a local war memorial. Sgt. Will Stones was shot for 'apparently' laying down his weapon in the face of the enemy. His family had been spearheading a national pardon campaign. When Will's name was belatedly added to the memorial, we felt that this was a story people would want to find out more about. Schools were keen to engage in the project, partly because of the success of *The Bonny Moorhen*, but also because of links with Modern History and English Literature study of the War Poets.

We knew we needed to engage with the energy of the young people. We decided to use a mix of creative writing, drama and dance in our schools workshops, emulating scenes from the play which was largely set at a tea dance. The dramatist, Dave Napthine, used a series of flashbacks to unravel the complexities of the story, and so our workshop participants were guided to do the same. Creating plausible characters, they wrote imaginary letters from

PHOTO: HELEN WARD

the Front to Home and vice versa. Using letter fragments as spoken text, the young people then created a dance routine featuring the Charleston, the Lambeth Walk and other dances from the early 1920's. This was performed for parents and friends on *The Set in Stone* set. People then stayed to watch the play, intrigued to find out about something which had already touched their hearts through the council's decision to add Will Stones' name to the memorial.

Teachers discovered too, that the drama and characterisation work had given the young people a licence to explore deep emotions and had helped them find ways of expressing these in words. Fictitious letters written by pupil participants (aged thirteen to sixteen) were very moving. Of particular note was the raw emotional quality of the boys' writing, something that is not generally evident in their day-to-day English work.

Here is a piece written by an average ability Year 11 pupil.

Dear Jennifer.

Only one more week till I see your beautiful smile again. Once more my heart chimes like on those hot summer days when we walked in the park like

young love-birds. Tomorrow we are going to the front-line to see how the old chaps are getting on and that should be our last duty before we leave. Till next week keep my love inside your heart, and remember I love you.
Ernest.

The Third Play

Arch Enemies: Our final play in the County Durham local history trilogy was inspired by the building of Causey Arch, the oldest railway bridge in the world. For this piece we returned to playwright Jim Woodland, knowing that he could deliver not only a play based on excellent research into industrial archaeology, but also write us some cracking good songs! We also decided to return to the workshop model we had used for *The Bonny Moorhen*, which would use drama workshops initially as a means of exploring social and political history with Key Stage 3 pupils, and then culminate with a carnival type happening for the entertainment and amusement of the general public.

Arch Enemies was set on top of the parapet on the day of the Grand Opening of the bridge in 1720. Our workshop participants therefore recreated the eighteenth-century street fair that would have undoubtedly accompanied such a momentous occasion. The story of Causey Arch is steeped in mystery and intrigue due to the fact that the bridge's master-mason Ralph Wood was found dead in the gorge below. Wood reputedly jumped to his death, plagued by fears that his structure was unsound. Jim Woodland's script played up the murder mystery element of the story – with the Spirit of the Bridge masquerading as a troublesome lad throughout, only revealing itself in the final eerie moments of the play.

The young people had the chance to play key characters in the story (many of them drawn from real life). They were then asked to make up their own minds about what had happened to Wood. Their theories were diverse, ranging from: 'he slipped and fell because he was drunk', to 'he was pushed by another stone-mason jealous of his achievement'. In the final sessions, participants were asked to create street characters with wares to sell and entertainment to offer. These included performing animals and human freaks, disreputable tinkers, prize-fighters, fortune-tellers, quack doctors and dancing girls. We provided costumes and props, with the young people making additional items.

In one school, we ran extra workshops, introducing the pupils to our set-designer, who helped them to design, and make scale models for street stalls.

The workshop process helped to create an enormous buzz in all of the schools. When the actors arrived to assemble the set for each evening's performance they were met with hordes of willing pupils desperate to help unload the van! As with *The Bonny Moorhen* the performances took place in a lively atmosphere, very different from that of a conventional theatre space. At times, it seemed as if the audience would never be quiet enough for the play to begin. The actors could sense a wildness in the air, and we acknowledged the potential danger of the situation. The play had a complex story-line. It was littered with obscure historical references and engineering jargon. If we failed to take our audience with us on this roller-coaster journey, they would certainly vote with their feet (and their rough quick wit) – parents and children alike. As well as the schools performances, we toured *Arch Enemies* to small-scale theatres and arts centres, village halls and community centres. Overall it was a very successful tour, but the gigs that stick in the actors' minds are the schools' shows for young audiences – where history really came to life!

School and Community Audiences Linked

The company performances in schools, and informal educational settings, had a preceding practical workshop. Young people often continued, through joining our evening Youth Theatre groups, and attending our Summer Schools. The school workshop sessions led to a presentation of their own work on the project theme. Friends and family who came along to enjoy the young people's early evening performances, then stayed to watch the Jack Drum main show.

Through the theatre for young people we had created a community audience. There had been no audience-building models for us to follow. Perhaps this is a 'theatre of stealth'?

Julie Ward co-founded the Jack Drum Arts in 1986 after working in the community for Northern Shape. She has received awards for her pioneering work in making the arts accessible in marginalized communities.

9. ACROSS THE TWO BRANCHES
Art Form and Educational

Two long-established companies with a record of producing innovative, high quality work in both branches of young people's theatre – the artistic and the educational.

PERFORMANCE AND WORKSHOP THEATRE

Mike Dalton explains the links between Pop-up as a performance company and its development of cutting-edge educational workshops run by actors.

Pop-up has pioneered high quality productions which explore important issues in children's lives, and has stimulated other areas of exploration. The company has two main arms:

- **Children's Theatre.** Original productions each year for children (under twelves) and adults. Touring theatres, schools and other venues.
- **Equal Voice.** A programme of combining actors in school and drama workshops for young people, and teachers. It develops self-esteem and explores ways of communicating and developing new life skills. These developments have been directly inspired by the ventures we have undertaken and the realisations they stimulated.

How we started – from the 'Mechanical' to the 'Emotional'

In 1982, with a mechanical table-top set used by one actor to create a performance for under five year-olds – 'pop up' – was what things did on the set. Part of the fascination of the first shows was mechanical intrigue – how did the flowers grow? – the chameleon change colour? the kangaroo row a boat? – the penguin skate on ice? We provided a little visual magic to drive the story on. Because it was successful we enlarged the sets and used more actors. We discovered that, despite maintaining the 'fascination of the mechanical', something else was becoming even more intriguing to the audience, and to us – the emotion of the stories, the relationships, and the drama as presented by the actors. We experimented a lot with the style, content and location of productions; physical, multi-media, non-verbal, outdoor. We worked closely with David Almond developing *Wild Girl, Wild Boy* and after the success of the production again worked with him to adapt his acclaimed novel *Heaven Eyes.*

Pop-Up productions are always non-prescriptive, and never promote a message of education or behaviour. Our show about sibling rivalry for Under-5's shows a young person loving a new brother but also feeling pushed out and resentful. The audience can empathise, especially if they felt mixed and confusing emotions about their own brothers or sisters. Before the show, they may sometimes have wished that their sibling didn't exist, perhaps even feeling guilty at such inexplicable thoughts. Afterwards, they would at least know that they are not alone. It's a normal and common reaction. That is the power of theatre for the young; by actually showing and having feelings, they understand it more. How else would they do it? Four year-olds don't sit together discussing their confusing emotions. We would never present a play to give ways you should tolerate a new baby, deal with a bully, behave in a school. The list goes on, with the word 'should' in front of it. We want to explore, not present an answer. We do not just choose plays that are 'saying something' but, make sure that the emotional conflict is relevant, and within the experience of our audience.

PHOTO: WAYNE PARRY

Starry Starry Night

School Performance

One of our priorities in designing new shows for Under-8's is to be compact enough for a school, but big enough for theatre, and look good in both. Our productions in schools are often a young person's first experience of theatre. We make lighting, sound and design transform a school hall into a theatre environment. They file in and sit on the floor of the school hall, a bench if they're lucky. The same anticipation and excitement that can be felt in a theatre. The familiar environment has changed, music is playing, the lights are low, and something is going to happen.

The only way that you would know the performance is for children is from the story and the dynamics on stage. We ensure that we do not have actors talking in a 'childish' voice, physicalising in a knock-knee'd way, or exaggerating facial gestures as if to say 'I'm very young'. That's like performing with a jokey Irish accent in Dublin – insulting.

The music fades, the play begins, seizes the school audience's attention and, hopefully, the attention of those teachers sitting at the sides who are only watching the children. The story unfolds, the characters develop, the audience gradually become as one, silent or laughing, gasping or calling out. They have permission to relax and watch; nothing is expected of them. This is especially important for a first-time theatre audience. Sometimes, especially with younger audiences, there is no applause until the actors come on to take their bow. It's not instinctive to applaud at the end of a play, because hopefully there is more. The actors coming on together says that it's over. Then it is instinctive to show appreciation – if deserved. We do not talk to audiences afterwards. We want to preserve a true theatrical experience. The audience leave, back to their classrooms and within an hour the company, the set, the lights and equipment have gone. The hall is bare without even marks from the gaffer tape that held down the floor-cloth.

Children's and Family Shows

All of our projects are concerned with seeing the world through young people's eyes, and trying to provide something they have not previously experienced. We produce shows for children and family shows. The difference is that the family show might deal with communication between young and old or attitudes to young people.

PHOTO: RICHARD KEEP

Family scene

Our Second Arm – We develop a Workshop Programme

When we performed in schools we were often asked to carry out a follow-up workshop with a class or classes. It was hard enough to get high quality actors to go on the road together for months – but did they have the skills to take workshops delving into the hidden mysteries of the play or the secrets of theatre? In 1991, we created a programme run by professional facilitators using drama as a tool for personal expression.

The Equal Voice programme works with young people using drama-based exercises to create safety and equality for all participants. This safe space allows young people to be able to look at their behaviour, experiment and make appropriate changes if they want to. The programme began by looking at self-esteem in situations of conflict and it initiated a learning process that has not diminished. As we defined conflict, we came to understand that it could include learning to tie a shoelace or to shape letters and numbers. We realised that all learning is conflict, and so schools should be full of it, celebrating it and dealing with it creatively. Self-esteem can be badly bruised when we struggle with conflict and we feel that we have not dealt with it well. That gave us our initial mission, to create an environment where self-esteem is not lowered in situations of conflict. After all, conflict is an opportunity for choice and change, let's promote it. We raised funds from charitable foundations and education authorities. We were specifically asked by funders to look at an area of teacher concern – bullying in schools.

An EQUAL Voice

We wanted everybody involved to have an effective voice, and looked closely at the way we structured our workshops. We found that many 'drama-based' games and exercises depend on quick thinking, quick moving, support of friends, particular skills or being chosen to take part. As a simple example, the children's party game Musical Chairs, or Musical Bumps, could not be an Equal Voice game. There is one winner and many losers, and once you are a loser you take no further part in the game. Why are you there? – to watch the winner. We were used extensively in trouble spots by schools and education authorities. We were successful and eased situations by getting pupils to devise dramas to experiment with new ways of relating.

However, we realised lasting change could only come from teachers making Equal Voice integral to all aspects of education. Teachers became our priority. We know they, like anybody, can feel nervous about running drama-based sessions. We provided a *Handbook of Games and Techniques*, with an introduction video. How to set up a safe space with clear rules and boundaries; success only being measured by the effective involvement of all participants. The priority in any session is that there are no judgements, no put downs, no being left out and, especially, no chance of failure. It is about speaking for yourself, being heard with respect and hearing others with respect.

Mark the Mood – A School Project

Dramatic Presentation. First the two Equal Voice leaders give an entertaining dramatic presentation with the whole school assembled, illustrating the four behaviour types that cover everything that happens in a school. It is a presentation without props, costumes, floor-cloths or lights. The audience see the two performers spin around once, describe themselves as being ten year-olds, and tell us about their family and their pets. We then discover that these two best friends are in dispute about the ownership of a kitten ('That's my cat, he ran away' – 'I saved his life, you don't deserve him'). The audience are encouraged to give their opinion as to who should have the cat, and it's not easy. The performers spin again, and we are into something completely new, an argument about whose idea something was ('She said my picture was best' – Only because I let you use my silver pen'). It is fast, funny and true.

The audience then help set up scenes for the actors to act out. Somebody being left out, or whispered about. They laugh, even though it's painful to see, and they empathise with the excluded. The actors ask the audience – 'Has that ever happened to you?' and a sea of hands confirms its relevance. Name-calling and insults – 'Where did you get those trainers?' – 'You can't even write properly' – 'What did you say about my mum!' Bullying – 'Do it, now!' Volunteers act

Discussion group

out being made to break a school window, or having their money taken. The performers quickly cover a whole range of incidents, and finally describe the four behaviour types that have been shown. It is fast moving and, unlike our theatre, a participatory experience.

Afterwards every pupil completes a simple questionnaire to identify which of the behaviours they would most like to lose in their class. They go back to their classrooms knowing they will be working with us, knowing they will have a chance to 'perform' in the same way and watch a video of young people carrying out the techniques. We run an introductory session for teachers, share the questionnaire results to help identify the current class issues, and identify the focus of the initial workshop sessions.

Classroom Session

We begin with the class in a circle. We work together so everyone is emotionally and physically safe, listening, being heard and respectful of other's opinions. Drama games encourage eye contact, emotional expression and mixing of the group without winners or losers. In small groups, the pupils are given a title to improvise and they act out a thirty second drama related to the questionnaire. For example, if the main issue is 'being left out', the drama scene title might be – Can I Play? Sometimes pupils, especially the younger ones, will just modify and repeat something from the assembly presentation. That doesn't matter because they are discovering a new way to display issues that affect them. When they have presented their story, we use various techniques.

I-time: saying 'I noticed... I think... I feel... I would be happier... I want...' individuals comment on what is happening to each person in a situation.

Circle-talk: collective solutions to an issue affecting the whole class, (e.g. boys not letting girls play football) are discussed in a seated circle.

Equal Voice is about the group developing greater responsibility and empathy for each other, being able to say how they want their class to be and taking pride in it. Equal Voice can focus on conflict, personal expression, trust, effective listening, communication, presentation and personal development.

What has Equal Voice to do with Theatre?

If theatre is not about conflict and emotion, it's not good theatre. If we don't know those conflicts and emotions, how can we make good theatre? Equal Voice involves us closely with the lives of our audience, their fears, traumas, problems. Because we can quickly develop emotionally articulate working relationships with young people, we can share that with other professionals.

Our National Lottery funded project, *Dramatic Links*, allowed us to put young people, a dramaturge and established playwrights who had not written for young people, together in Equal Voice workshops. The writers could communicate with young people from many cultures; they could talk and work equally, understand a modern childhood and not write, as a lot of writers do, just from the memory of their own childhood. It was a rewarding process that led to us commissioning and producing exciting new plays and one that we are now extending to include younger children. We don't have to justify Equal Voice any more; Dramatic Links has been used as a model by other theatre companies and our theatre work is always reaching into new areas. All of the understandings of behaviour; gained from working in primary schools, make good theatre, totally relevant and empowering.

We are currently developing a play about behaviour in primary schools – perhaps a continuing episodic soap – which will inform, entertain and may give us all fresh insights into the daily dramas of school life. Young people's theatre can be a lonely world when there is not collaboration between artists in different fields or in different sectors of theatre. We are currently bringing together artists from all areas for collaborative workshops to develop new productions. We've started the development workshops in different cities and already have a wide and wild range of ideas and art forms. We are taking Equal Voice to New Zealand. The lower recorded attainment of Maori young people in schools is very similar to the situation of Afro-Caribbean young people in England. We have experience in this field, and are funded to work on both the North and South Island.

Whatever form these projects take, we know that the experience of carrying them out will stimulate and develop new theatre passions and activities.

Mike Dalton is Director of Pop-up Theatre and has developed a wide range of children and young people's theatre projects.

EDUCATIONAL AND ART FORM THEATRE

David Farmer describes the original TIE company-devised educational theatre, and the move into creating original imaginative theatre, demonstrating company commitment to high quality work in both branches of theatre for young people.

The past few years have seen Tiebreak moving away from its origins as part of the British Theatre-in-Education movement, away from issue-based plays and workshops, to performances where the enjoyment of live theatre is the primary objective.

The company was set up in 1981 by a teacher and a drama advisor (Jon Oram and myself), with no funding or financial support, based at Norwich Arts Centre. Early work was a mixture of devised plays with participatory workshops. Myself and three other 'actor-teachers' wrote the plays, built the sets, made the costumes, marketed the productions, phoned the schools, drove the van and performed in a hundred and fifty shows each year. Initially, we had to charge schools for visits as we had no Education Authority support. Finally, Eastern Arts Board started to award the company project grants.

When devising work, we would sit and draft educational objectives, and a list of scenes on a blackboard, then get up and improvise action and dialogue. Often scenes were recorded onto a simple tape-machine, and redrafted by the group into a script. The method was successful. We would take it in turn to stand outside the action, and give advice in rehearsal. Once or twice an outside director was brought in, although that role was not usually considered necessary. This co-operative approach was taken by many companies at the time. Directors were seen as a threat to the communal ensemble approach.

Socially-aware Theatre

We toured plays to children of all school ages, from five to eighteen. In line with much other contemporary TIE, themes centred around social history and social issues; plays about the peasants' revolt, striking farm-workers, prisons and the Poor Law. Whatever the subject, a left-wing approach was taken to the work, influenced by the early repercussions of Thatcherism.

The Burston School Strike, a Norfolk local history story. Parents and school children went on strike in 1914 to protest against child labour exploitation on the farms. *The Burston Story* was staged in the round, with the children sitting on the floor, the action taking place in and amongst them. This took advantage of the open space of the school hall and enabled a deep level of emotional involvement by audience members, with flexible stage movement by the three actors. A 'hot-seating' session followed the play, during which children would question the characters individually about their motives and the social issues.

Curriculum Context

After the introduction of the National Curriculum in 1987, Tiebreak provided plays which matched particular Curriculum Key Stage objectives. Contemporary social issues were explored, including prejudice, anti-racism, feminism, attitudes to disability, integrated theatre for the deaf, conservation, the heritage industry and juvenile crime. With all of the productions, we worked closely with a voluntary Teachers' Panel, as well as advisors from the Education Authority. The company now operated on a project basis, and commissioned external writers. PSHE is a key part of the National Curriculum. Norfolk Action Against AIDS and the Arts Council helped finance one of the first TIE plays about HIV/AIDS.

Love Bites by Leslie Davidoff: used irreverent humour, provocative performances and loud music to grab the attention of its teen audience in schools and youth clubs. The four teenage characters – one gay lad, one girl dabbling in drugs, a Jack-the-lad who slept around, and a naïve virgin on the verge of sleeping with her boyfriend – helped to highlight a variety of attitudes toward HIV.

Dramatic highlights included the sensitive coming out of the gay young man, and the subsequent physical attack by his best mate, an argument over the refusal to carry condoms in a handbag, and comedic scenes taking place in fast-food joints, a disco and alongside the school play. The multi-layered issues again led to lively 'hot-seating' sessions. The actors learnt quickly that to grab attention in youth clubs, the more sexuality and swearing the better. This did not go down well when they returned to the school environment. One hot-seating session was

PHOTO: RICHARD DENYER

Love Bites

stopped in mid-flow, and the company sent packing by a deputy head (due to Jack-the-lad's gratuitous use of four-letter words). However the production proved enormously popular, and was toured for five years, with many schools basing their entire year's Personal, Social and Health Education on *Love Bites*.

Company Development

This was an active period for the company, and its reach was extended beyond schools as a wider range of organisations turned to theatre as an alternative educational tool. A productive period followed with plays being commissioned for Norfolk Health Authority, the Colchester Museum, Norfolk Museums, Forest Enterprise and Lynx Animal Rights Campaign. The work produced was reactive, responding to the needs of the institutions. Plus shows in London at the Unicorn Theatre and at festivals in Canada and the USA. This was in addition to the regular programme of theatre for schools in East Anglia. International touring is time-consuming on an administrative level so Tiebreak focused its energies back in the UK. We now produced more work for a younger age group (5 to 8 years). This freed the company from the stricter demands of the National Curriculum, and enabled us to concentrate more on theatre as art form than educational tool.

We also now found an increasing demand from theatres and art centres. Up to now, we had rarely performed in designated buildings, enjoying the challenge of non-theatre spaces and the experience of working with audiences, many of whom would probably never set foot inside a theatre. However, as awareness of the educational needs of younger children developed nationally, art centres were finding more demand from parents for theatre aimed at young audiences. This created a further impetus in the development of the company. Tiebreak continued school touring with venue performances taking place at weekends.

Then a final break with issue-led work came in the late 1990's. Our productions now used physical theatre, comedy and live music. Visits to international festivals of theatre for young people in Belgium, France, Germany and Cuba provided strong influences, along with inspiring examples of physical theatre in the UK, from leading companies, such as Theatre de Complicité and Trestle Theatre.

Suitcase full of Stories: used a physicalised storytelling approach to explore world folk tales. A grumpy removal man and his young assistant are clearing out a dusty old attic when they come across a suitcase which seems to have a mind of its own. On opening the case, its contents are removed one by one, each object proving itself to be a key element in a story. The spirits of the stories take control of the two labourers as they re-enact each story, using the bric-a-brac around them to conjure up images.

A ghostly puppet is slowly assembled, and brought to life, as a lonely old woman sings a song about her strange visitor whilst spinning wool (on a bicycle wheel). A bouncy yellow ball becomes the sun in a fable about the strongest person in the world, with dances to a bhangra backing and jive.

A Suitcase full of Stories

Tubing from an old tumble drier becomes the stretchy trunk in a tug-of-war between a hippopotamus and an elephant. Much of the action took place without words to a background fusion of world music. The strong visual content and humour had a wide appeal to the young audiences.

Whilst such productions were motivated more by an exploration of theatrical technique and storytelling, themes from plays were still explored in an educational context. Using the expertise of external advisors, we continued to produce Teachers' Resource Packs to support the experience of live theatre.

As well as working with outside writers such as Neil Duffield and Robert Rigby, Tiebreak began adapting well-known stories and books for the younger age group such as *Frog in Love* by Max Velthuijs and *One Dark Night*, by Mike Kenny, a collection of world stories and music. Writing and devising with the actors enabled him to further develop his own approach to the work, exploring the theatrical dimension of tried and tested stories as well as a more collaborative approach in rehearsals. He also began composing some music and songs himself in addition to working with other composers.

Artistic Collaboration

I had long known the work of Hoipolloi Theatre, and the Le Coq Theatre School. The company had moved to Cambridge, and developed a physical theatre and comedy approach through shows which they toured throughout the UK, and internationally. Although their work was aimed at young adult audiences, much of their style appealed to younger children. With this in mind the two companies discussed a touring show which would be suitable for both adults and children. I had been looking at the writing of Edward Lear, the writer of nonsense poems, and felt that his life and work would provide a suitable vehicle for both companies to collaborate on.

The show would tour to theatres throughout the UK – not to schools. This would enable a full lighting design, and a larger cast and set than would normally be possible. The directors of each company collaborated on the research into Lear's nonsense writing and drawings, as well as joint workshops and auditions as the performing company was put together. They co-wrote the production.

My Uncle Arly: This is a markedly different show to any that Tiebreak had previously been involved with. Using physical theatre, object animation, mime, song and clowning, this is a total theatre performance. The words and characters invented by Edward Lear provide the backdrop to a journey by the Victorian writer and artist. With the action framed by a miniature proscenium arch, Uncle Arly (Edward Lear's alter-ego) is seen taking his leave of friends as he sets out on a journey across France and Italy to paint.

From this point, the grotesque words and creatures from Lear's imagination take centre-stage as easels, walking sticks, top hats, blocks of wood, leather bags and even a stuffed cat. Through highly choreographed ensemble playing we lose touch with cosy Victoriana, and are transported deeper into Lear's dark imaginings. This production was the result of a collaborative process between the two companies, actors, writers, director, composer and designers, enabling the fullest use of every resource.

The aim of *My Uncle Arly* was to provide audiences with the most creative and imaginative show possible. It worked extremely well for the target audience of eight year-olds to adult. Staging the play at the Edinburgh Festival led to admiring reviews, award nominations and an appearance at the Royal Opera House Festival of Firsts. This has led to invitations to work abroad, as well as raising the profile of children's theatre on a national level.

Tiebreak Today

Tiebreak has come a long way since its early days as is reflected in the style, content and theatre-based audience of *My Uncle Arly*. Indicative of this change in direction, the company has found a new home in an active theatre – Norwich Playhouse. However Tiebreak has not forgotten its most important audience – the company plans to continue balancing its work in schools with national venue touring and co-producing with theatres.

David Farmer has directed both forms of Tiebreak Theatre's work.

10. TOURING THEATRE FOR FAMILY AUDIENCES

There is a wide range of innovative companies who tour the network of small theatre and local venues, presenting theatre for family and young audiences, using visual and physical theatre to stimulate the imaginations and feelings. Here are brief programme descriptions of some of the many companies currently touring to Arts Centres and Community Venues.

Action Transport (Midlands) – www.actiontransporttheatre.co.uk

Theatre which amazes, enriches and sometimes changes lives. With Vulavulani Theatre (Soweto), a folk tale comes alive. Tselani and Monkey have to outwit Lion and Thunder Giant.

Cahoots NI Theatre (Belfast) – www.cahootsni.com

Theatre to expand children's creativity in all communities. Bedside Theatre – 5 minute plays for children in hospital wards.

Cornelius and Jones (Midlands) – www.corneliusjones.com

Creating original and dynamic theatre for children.Toy Theatre – paper puppets come to life in a busy Victorian street.

Kazzum (London-based) – www.kazzum.org

Visual theatre, masks, puppets to create original productions and installations. And classic world stories like Pinocchio.

Konflux Theatre (York) – www.konfluxtheatre.com

Interactive theatre to inspire imagination/creative learning. Charlie plays computer games, but meets real creatures in the garden, and goes underwater.

Magic Carpet (Hull)
www.magiccarpettheatre.com

Theatre using physical theatre, clown, magic and circus skills. The Ringmaster invites you to join the travelling circus.

M6 – Rochdale
www.m6theatre.co.uk

Danny, King of the Basement. Award-winning play from Roseneath Theatre Toronto. Danny and his mother move into his eight home, and he meets the local kids and makes friends

Magic Carpet

Ripstop (London-based)
www.ripstoptheatre.co.uk

Imaginative Shadow Puppet Theatre, live music and singing. The Jumblies leap from the pages of the book and go to sea in a sieve.

Ripstop

Theatre-rites (London-based)
www.theatre-rites.co.uk

Pushing back the boundaries of theatre form. Site-specific and touring shows. 'Let's make our own house!' says the child. Learning to play and make homes together.

A full list of member companies can be found on the ASSITEJ UK website

PLAYSCRIPTS AND PUBLICATIONS

Edward Bond *The Children* (Methuen) ISBN 0-413-75630-0

Leo Butler *Devotion* (Aurora Metro) ISBN 0-9542330-4-2

Noël Grieg *Trashed* (Aurora Metro) ISBN 0-9546912-2-9

David Holman *No Worries – Three Plays for Young People* (Currency Press, Sydney) ISBN 0-868190-181-7

Philip Ridley *Sparkleshank* (Samuel French) ISBN 0-573-05122-4

Simon Stephens *Herons* (Methuen) ISBN 0-413-76370-6

Charles Way *A Spell of Cold Weather* (Aurora Metro) ISBN 0-9542330-8-5

Charles Way *The Search for Odysseus – in Young Blood: 5 Plays for Young Performers* (Aurora Metro) ISBN 0-9515877-6-5

Charles Way *Plays for Young People* (Aurora Metro) ISBN 0-9536757-1-8

Jacqueline Wilson *Double Act* adapted by **Vicky Ireland**
(Collins Plays Plus) with notes ISBN 0-00717994-4
(Random House) Play Edition ISBN 0440866316

David Wood *Plays: Volume 1 and 2* (Methuen) ISBN 0-413-73700-4

Nick Wood *Warrior Square* (Aurora Metro) ISBN 0-9546912-0-2

Theatre Centre: Plays for Young People, Volume 1

Benjamin Zephaniah, Angela Turvey, Anna Reynolds, Anna Furse, Manjinder Virk, Roy Williams (Aurora Metro) ISBN 0-9542330-5-0

Teaching Resource Videos for Theatre Centre Plays Education Department
(www.theatre-centre.co.uk)

Theatre for Children – A Guide to Writing, Adapting, Directing and Acting
David Wood (Faber) ISBN 0-571-17749-2

Taking Issue – Three Playwrights and a Theatre Company

Mike Kenny, Mark Catley, Mary Cooper and Theatre Blah, Blah, Blah
(Alumnus Press) ISBN 1-901-439-03-8
Learning through Theatre edited by **Tony Jackson**
– New Perspectives on Theatre in Education (Routledge) ISBN 0-415-08609
DVD of *The Gruffalo* in performance

All available from: **London Drama Book Service – www.londondrama.org**

COMPANY CONTACTS AND WEBSITES

Jeremy Turner – Director
Arad Goch Theatre, Aberystwyth
+44 (0)1970 617998
jeremy@aradgoch.org
www.aradgoch.org
www.agordrysau-openingdoors.org

Steve Ball – Education Director
Birmingham Repertory Theatre
+44 (0)12 12452091
education@birmingham-rep.co.uk
www.birmingham-rep.co.uk

Claudette Bryanston – Co-Director
Classworks Theatre, Cambridge
+44 (0)1223 249100
info@classworks.org.uk
www.classworks.org.uk

Paul Harman – Director
CTC Theatre, Darlington
+44 (0)1325 352004
paul@ctctheatre.org.uk
www.ctctheatre.org.uk

Peter Rumney, Nettie Scriven
Dragon Breath, Nottingham
+44 (0) 1159 553493
dragonbreath.theatre@ntlworld.com
www.dragon-breath-theatre.co.uk

Julie Davies – Director
Gwent TIE, Abergavenny
+ 44 (0)1873 853167
gwentie@uwclub.net
www.gwenttie.co.uk

Tony Reekie – Director
Imaginate Festival, Edinburgh
+44 (0)131 225 8050
admin@imaginate.org.uk
www.imaginate.org.uk

Julie Ward – Director
Jack Drum Arts, South Durham
+ 44 (0)1833 696630
info@jackdrum.co.uk
www.jackdrum.co.uk

Dominic Rai – Director
Mán-Melá Asian Theatre
+44 (0)20 8983 9551
dominic@manmela.org.uk
www.manmela.org.uk

Andrew Breakwell – Director
Nottingham Playhouse
Roundabout TIE
+44 (0)1158 736230
admin@nottinghamplayhouse.co.uk
www.nottinghamplayhouse.co.uk

Tim Webb – Director
Oily Cart, London
+44 (0)20 8672 6329
oilies@oilycart.org.uk
www.oilycart.org.uk

Sarah Kettlewell – Administrator
Playtime Theatre Company, Kent
+44 (0)1227 266272
playtime@dircon.co.uk
www.playtime.dircon.co.uk

Annie Wood – Director
Stephen Midlane – Administrator
Richard Shannon – Playgrounding
Polka Theatre, South London
+44 (0)20 8545 4888
admin@polkatheatre.com
www.polkatheatre.com

Mike Dalton – Artistic Director
Pop-Up Theatre, North London
44 (0)20 7609 3339
admin@pop-up.net
www.pop-up.net
www.equalvoice.net

Carey English – Joint Director
Quicksilver Theatre, London
+ 44 (0)20 7241 2942
talktous@quicksilver.org
www.quicksilvertheatre.org

Richard Croxford – Artisitic Director
Replay Productions, Belfast
+44 (0)2890 322773
replay@dircon.co.uk
www.replayproductions.org

Philip Clark – Artistic Director
Margaret Jones – General Manager
Sherman Theatre, Cardiff
+44 (0) 2920 646901
gm@shermantheatre.demon.co.uk
www.shermantheatre.co.uk

Olivia Jacobs/Toby Mitchell –
Co-Directors
Tall Stories, London
+44 (0)20 8343 8527
tallstories@virgin.net
www.tallstories.org.uk

Rosamunde Hutt – Director
Thomas Kell – Administrator
Theatre Centre, London
+44 (0)20 7729 3066
admin@theatre-centre.co.uk
www.theatre-centre.co.uk

Anthony Haddon – Director
Theatre Blah Blah Blah, Leeds
+44 (0)113 224 3171
admin@blahs.co.uk
www.blahs.co.uk

Ian Yeoman – Director
Theatr Powys, Llandrindod Wells
+44 (0)1597 824444
admin@ntmail.powys.gov.uk
www.theatrpowys.co.uk

David Farmer – Director
Tiebreak Theatre, Norwich
+44 (0)1663 665899
admin@tiebreak-theatre.com
www.tiebreak-theatre.com

Jude Merrill – Artistic Producer
Cath Gregg – General Manager
Travelling Light, Bristol
+44 (0)117 377 3166
info@travlight.co.uk
www.travlight.co.uk

Tony Graham – Artistic Director
Carl Miller – Literary Manager
Unicorn Theatre, London
+44 (0)20 7700 0702
admin@unicorntheatre.com
www.unicorntheatre.com

David Wood – Writer and Director
Whirligig Theatre
+44 (0)181 947 173
davidwoodplays@virgin.net
www.davidwood.org.uk

UK Branch of ASSITEJ
www.assitejuk.org

International ASSITEJ
www.assitej.org

KEY TERMS (covering the range of theatre activity)

PROFESSIONAL THEATRE

- **Children's Theatre:** performance for children under 11.
- **Young People's Theatre (YPT):** performance for over 11 to 18's.
- **Theatre-in-Education (TIE):** Actor-Teachers using participatory drama and theatre in school.

SCHOOL DRAMA:

- **Drama-in-Education (DIE):** Teacher-led role-play to explore a learning area in groups.
- **Drama:** Devised and text performance as school subject.
- **School Productions:** Young people performing a play, for a school and parent audience.
- **Youth Theatre:** Young people performing a play.

CHILDREN'S THEATRE FESTIVALS

Take Off	Darlington/North East *(www.ctctheatre.org)*
Spark	Leicester/Midlands *(www.spart.co.uk)*
Ciao	Bracknell/South East *(www.ciaofestival.org)*
Agor Drysau	Aberystwyth, Wales
Opening Doors	*(www.agordrysau-opening doors.org)*
Imaginate	Edinburgh *(www.imaginate.org.uk)*
Young at Art	Belfast, Northern Ireland *(www.youngatart.co.uk)*

aurora metro press

Founded in 1989 to publish and promote new writing, the press has specialized in new drama, fiction and work in translation, winning recognition and awards from the industry.

New drama
I have before me a remarkable document...
by Sonja Linden **ISBN 0-9546912-3-7 £7.99**

Harvest by Manjula Padmanabhan
ISBN 0-9536757-7-7 £6.99

Under Their Influence by Wayne Buchanan
ISBN 0-9536757-5-0 £7.99

Trashed by Noël Greig
ISBN 0-9546912-2-9 £7.99

Lysistrata - the sex strike by Aristophanes, adapted by Germaine Greer and Phil Willmott **ISBN 0-9536757-0-8 £7.99**

Anthologies
Six plays by Black and Asian women writers
ed. Kadija George **ISBN 0-9515877-2-2 £11.99**

Black and Asian plays introduced by Afia Nkrumah
ISBN 09536757-4-2 £9.95

Seven plays by women, female voices, fighting lives
ed. Cheryl Robson **ISBN 0-9515877-1-4 £5.95**

A touch of the Dutch: plays by women
ed. Cheryl Robson **ISBN 0-9515877-7-3 £9.95**

Mediterranean plays by women
ed. Marion Baraitser **ISBN 0-9515877-3-0 £9.95**

Eastern Promise, *7 plays from central and eastern Europe*
eds. Sian Evans and Cheryl Robson **ISBN 0-9515877-9-X £11.99**

www.aurorametro.com